ARCHING
BACKWARD

ARCHING BACKWARD

The Mystical Initiation of a Contemporary Woman

JANET ADLER

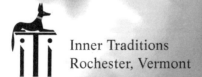

Inner Traditions
Rochester, Vermont

Inner Traditions International
One Park Street
Rochester, Vermont 05767

Library of Congress Cataloging-in-Publication Data
Adler, Janet.
Arching backward : the mystical initiation of a
contemporary woman/ Janet Adler.
p. cm.
ISBN 0-89281-577-9
1. Adler, Janet.   2. Spiritual biography—United States.   3. Visions.
4. Women and religion.   5. Initiation rites—Religious aspects.   I. Title.
BL 730.A25A3   1995
291.4'092–dc20
[B]   95–24266
CIP

Printed and bound in the United States

10 9 8 7 6 5 4 3 2 1

Text design and layout by Virginia L. Scott

Woodcuts by Phillip Buller

This book was typeset in Life with Trajan and Koch Antigua
as the display typefaces

Distributed to the book trade in Canada by Publishers Group West (PGW),
Toronto, Ontario

Distributed to the book trade in the United Kingdom by
Deep Books, London

Distributed to the book trade in Australia by Millennium Books, Newtown,
N.S.W.

Distributed to the book trade in New Zealand by
Tandem Press, Auckland

Distributed to the book trade in South Africa by
Alternative Books, Randburg

To Philip

In Gratitude

In Love

【】

CONTENTS

[ ]

ACKNOWLEDGMENTS

()

Profound gratitude is like mystical experience. Both are indescribable. Because in this context, words are my medium, the great depth of my appreciation becomes reflected in the beauty and simplicity of *thank you.*

Thank you Harriet Finkelstein, Rosalyn Driscoll, and Sibylle Baier for your soulful, compassionate, and clear presence from the beginning of my initiation to the publication of this text. *Thank you* Rosalind de Mille, Edith Sullwold, Alton Wasson, Anne Woodhull, Harriet Brickman, Joan Chodorow, Betsy Ellis-Kempner, Robert Lyons, Ingelisa, Daniel John, Michelle Beemer, Andrea Olsen, and Peter Schmitz. I often wonder what might have happened at the time of my initiation without my experience of your trust in me, your abundant generosity, your immediate presence in my life and the presence of many I do not name here.

Thank you Carolyn Sadeh, Nora Riley, Heidi Ehrenreich, Frances McKaig, Gwen Jenkins, Rosalind Fox, Sara White, Delyte Frost and Wendy Elliott, Susan Schell, Rose Mitchell, Anne Gosling-Goldsmith, Daphne Lowell, Mary Ramsey, and Joan Haefele Miller. My experience of your commitment to study at The Mary Starks Whitehouse Institute at the time of my initiation, your love, humor, and the gift of your work were profoundly related to my experiences.

Thank you Carol Barrett, Robert McAndrews, Caroline Schrodes, Ellen Colbert-Rohn, Fontaine Maury Belford, Elizabeth Petroff, Lee Sannella, Suzanne Lovell, Lisa Mertz, Frances Harwood, Jack Kornfield, Daniel Matt, and Patti Philo. You offered invaluable guidance within my doctoral studies at The Union Institute regarding my need to place my initiation experience in an historical context.

Thank you Ruthlee Adler, Sherry Anderson, Zoe Avstreih, Lisa Bourgea, Jeanne Castle, Nan Dale, Fran Dayan, Lori Delmartini Trew, Laurie Emerson, Sandy Dibbell-Hope, Lee Fuller, Lynn Fuller, Ellen Friedman, Deborah Gravelle, Susan Gregory, Terry Gregory, Neala Haze, Ellen Ketchum, Virginia King, Russell Lockhart, Bonney Lynch, JoEllen McNeal, Kathee Miller, Sara Norwood Hurley, Judy Orloff, Judith Peterman, Margaret Sekijima, Marg Starbuck, Tina Stromsted, Corlene van Sluizer, and Ruth Zaporah. I experienced your strong and loving support at different stages in the long process of the integration of my initiatory experiences.

Thank you Elaine Buller, Kathleen Frazer, and Gunther Stuhlmann for your excellent editorial advice. To those of you at Inner Traditions International who have thoughtfully and generously carried my manuscript into book form, *thank you.* My experience with you individually and as a working collective has been deeply moving. *Thank you* Robin Dutcher-Bayer for recognizing, correctly receiving, and with great warmth, honoring *Arching Backward* in relationship to publication. *Thank you* Susan Davidson for your fine sensitivity, enthusiasm, and your clarity in relationship to the text. *Thank you,* Ehud Sperling, for your wisdom in refusing my pseudonym.

Thank you, my dedicated physicians: Lois Johnson, Bill Weintraub, Joel Alter, and Peter Madill. *Thank you* Mary Whitehouse and John Weir, my teachers, for my experience of your devotion to your work.

And to my parents, Posy Woolf Adler and Leon Adler, *thank you* for the privilege of growing from the richly textured ground you laid under me.

Thank you, Joshua. *Thank you,* Paul. My experience of your innocence, your wisdom, and your unquestioning love as you endured, witnessed, and anchored the entire process continues to fill me with awe, with profound gratitude.

Philip Buller, *thank you.* I cannot separate this story from my experience of the depth of your being, your infinite capacity to love.

FOREWORD

()

This extraordinary work is the personal account of a contemporary woman's experience of initiation. But unlike the classical experience of initiation that takes place within the protection of culture and society, Janet Adler went through her experience of purgation and illumination mostly alone. It is a story about suffering and insight, and when reading it, one cannot help reflect on the narratives of shamans and mystics who recount their harrowing trials.

Janet Adler is a dancer, and we enter her experience through her body. She writes as though the body tissues are speaking directly to the reader. Adler feels that the body is the text through which mystical visions arise, and she has faithfully recorded her experiences from the body, from the flesh, in such a way that the reader feels taken into the skin, bones and marrow of the poetry of death and resurrection.

I met Janet Adler at the beginning of her initiatic journey. A strikingly beautiful woman, she moved with a freedom and depth that stopped this viewer's breath. Her thick brown hair and translucent smooth body was electric and subtle. Her face was full of wonder and pain. A spirit was before us, a soul being crafted by its very gestures. Her body was poetry in motion. On reading the remarkable account of her visions and journey, I see that the inside and outside have merged in her narrative. Like her dance, the text that we read is an emanation of a boundariless continuum, an ocean of suffering and poetry that has no horizon, a place that as well is stillness in motion.

Today, there are few refuges for those crossing the great river of change. For Adler, her refuge and healing has been the practice of writing. We too are the recipients of this gift; we are given refuge, an island of beauty to abide on as she moves through her story, her life, her text of embodied suffering and wisdom.

Joan Halifax

PROLOGUE

( )

Now comes the dawn, winter dawn. As I prepare to offer this book about my direct experience of the Mysteries, I can feel that the very energy that so fiercely initiated me is moving in me again this morning. Once more my movements slow down, the pressure behind my eyes pushes forward. I leave all that surrounds me—the rain boots, the dog bowls, the white flowers on the round table in the center of our home, three stems arching out from the blue vase. Lighting the candle as the pressure builds, I step into the hot bath. The water is my medium. The heat, the fluidity, the weight open me.

As I sit down in the water, I look through the glass doors into the back patio. I see the doves, the one white lily, just opening below the ivy-covered cage. We came here toward a wider sky nine years ago, seeking an open landscape to reflect my developing inner sense of emptiness, a vastness, created by my experience of this energy. Our house here receives the light everywhere, so different from the other house where this all began fifteen years ago within the protection, the darkness of New England's traditions.

This primal energy that has been moving within me, has a name in most cultures, and thus is recognized and integrated into the language, the psyche itself. It is called *n/um* by the !Kung tribe in Africa, *tum-mo* by the Tibetans, *huo* by the Taoists, *quaumaneq* by the Eskimos, *ch'i* by the Chinese, *kundalini* by the Hindus, *ki* by the Japanese. I can only call it energy, because we have no name for this phenomenon in the West.

For reasons that I do not understand, my nervous system translates this energy into visions. During my initiation, between 1981 and 1986, when such energy spontaneously entered and dominated my life, I received hundreds of visions reflecting archetypal images from several mystical traditions. Visions are different from my dreams because they directly affect my consciousness, occurring when I am awake. They are different from my experience of fantasy because they are made of light or electrical energy. The unusual visual clarity heightens my experience of the imagery as it burns, like fire, within my body.

What a great longing I have had to describe these indescribable experiences of vision—an unending paradox. I know it is the direct impact of the energy, not the visions themselves, that has irrevocably changed my life, yet I feel compelled to record them immediately after they occur, no matter what the circumstances. I write because of a persistent "knowing" that I must, with no embellishment, translate each vision into words. Perhaps I do this to simply bring into form that which originates in formlessness. Perhaps I write words in an effort to help me contain the experience. Perhaps the writing is an expression of hope, hope of communicating, and therefore reducing the loneliness that such experiences create.

Beneath the "knowing" to write in this way is another subtle knowing. Though direct experience of the numinous happens within my body, causing me to perceive life in a completely new way, it is not about me, it is not mine. My body is a conduit for energy destined for the collective body. Since the first vision, I have known, though not known how, that a text must be published. Containing it until now has been imperative. Publishing it, with deep ambivalence, has been inevitable. The experience is inseparable from the offering.

I know that translating the embodiment of these visions into words by tracking the experience is a way of witnessing myself, helping me to stay in a negotiating relationship to the energy rather than to merge with it. I know I am writing sensations vastly beyond accurate description, but my longing to move closer to a truer reflection of my experience is uncompromising. I long to write in a language that embodies the Mysteries, to write the experience rather than to write about it. Thus this text, this offering, is by necessity spare and by definition inadequate.

Though my relationship with the energy is profoundly intimate, each time I notice its presence, I am again innocent, not knowing, deeply respectful. I have chosen to fully receive it at this moment as there is space in my teaching practice—there is time before my responsibilities to the outside world begin once more. In this early morning vision, it is apparent that *Arching Backward* is published.

> **[O]** *Sitting on a stack of my journals in which the visions are written, I am being burned alive, not by the fire within but by a fire outside me, ignited and fueled by a deter-mined unconscious, by a white people who don't under-stand. I see them watching me burn.*

I realize that what happens now in this instant, being misunderstood and thus destroyed, has been an irrepressible fear since the beginning of my initiation. I must be experiencing the perseverance of a cellular memory, a shadow of Western religion's relationship to the mystic.

> **[O]** *I see a circle of women and men, mystics who were also burned in this way, standing behind these people who must destroy me. Transparent beings, they are containing, encircling my final burning. Their presence is humbling, helping me to stay in correct relationship to the changing of my form. While I am burning to white bone, those who destroy me with fire step backward into the circle of those who, because of fire, manifest compassion. Becoming one circle, I cannot tell the difference between those who burn and those who have been burned.*

I experience the timing of this vision as uncanny, as is often the case.

Central in my relationship to these occurrences has been my awareness
of and my respect for the organic and sequential order of the content of
the visions. When I am living in correct relationship to this process,
honoring the demand toward impeccability, I glimpse a synchronicity
between the content of the visions and the unfolding of my life.

Yet I knew from the first vision that the content was not about my
personal history, to be analyzed within any psychological framework.
Because of the preceding ten years of practice of Authentic Movement, a
movement discipline that concerns the complex and developing relationship between moving and witnessing, the nature of my experience of the
visions was that of receiving them, witnessing them, without interpreta-
tion or judgment and without intention to direct or control them.
Instead of perceiving the content of the visions from a psychological
perspective, the word mystical appeared in my mind as spontaneously as
the initiation itself, though I had no cognitive understanding of its
meaning, its history, or its roots.

In ancient traditions the embodiment of this energy created sacred
experiences that were contained within the ritual and practice of the
specific tribe, temple, or ashram. Today, in the lives of many Westerners
like me, there is an absence of a living circle, a community in which the
spiritual life of the individual is at the center. The absence of a teacher,
a language, symbols or texts, a sanctuary or an elder circle magnified
my aloneness and my vulnerability. As a marginal Jewess, my connection
to a spiritual collective was invisible, the lineage increasingly inacces-
sible. And my body, a woman's body, has historically been mostly
invisible as a vessel for holding such direct experience of spirit.

Paradoxically, I had no religious beliefs, no meditation practice, yet I
was having a profoundly religious experience in the historical sense of
that term. Though I believe we are currently experiencing a shift in the
relationship between religion and mysticism in the postmodern, Western
world, mystical experience has tenaciously and for centuries been
described within the context of organized religion.

I knew very little of the philosophies and histories of the world's
religions and nothing of mystical traditions. Neither the concept of
spiritual seeking nor the desire for spiritual experience was in my
conscious awareness at the time that my initiation began. I had no God

who intended this great change within me, who chose me to be challenged in this way or to be graced by such a gift. From my perspective, this particular energetic phenomenon is metaphysical, its potential existing in every person. My experience teaches me that it comes into existence because of the movement of a specific vibrational energy field in the universe, mysteriously touching the vibration of that same energy within a human being. This fusion occurred within my body, creating my devotion to a path of not knowing, yet trusting, a path of direct, embodied experience of a divine energy.

Because of the considerable force that this energy can manifest, psychosis and death are two major dangers inherent in initiatic journeys. I am grateful that psychosis was not a threat to me, perhaps because of the in-depth work I had done as a client in psychotherapy as a younger woman and as a movement therapist for the preceding fifteen years. Such continuous immersion in the ongoing engagement between body and psyche helped me, when I became an initiate, to maintain clear boundaries in terms of ego-consciousnesss, thus protecting me from identifying with the images in the visions, from psychological disturbance.

But death became an active, consistent companion. As though with intention to change my form, it entered my body through the direct impact of the energy itself and it entered my mind through recurring themes in the vision imagery. Because penetration of the energy occurred so rapidly, so fiercely, and without enough respite between rounds, the depletion of my physical body became a serious problem, a problem that at times became life threatening. A welcomed paradox: I experienced the grace of not having to literally die in order to change form.

Surviving and knowing I had to understand what happened to me, I returned from the intensity of such experiences with a great and ancient need to offer back. A mystical journey belongs to the culture in which it is seeded. The process of return was in itself a paradox because I was always returning to a self that I experienced as new, the old form continually burning away. When I became strong enough, after several years of rest, recovery, and integration, I turned to the writing of mystics to embrace me. Ultimately doctoral work in mystical studies offered me the necessary context within which I could place my personal experiences.

Discovering the correct context enabled me to imagine this text safely received by the contemporary culture in which I live.

It was then that I found the other essential element of my return. I discovered the form that organically and thus correctly manifests my experiences, this book. It is a weave of two narratives, of ordinary and nonordinary realities gleaned from journal entries from the initiation years. I remember the moment when I saw an image of my journal recordings of my experiences of the numinous, the visions themselves, pouring down over the edge of the right margin into columns. Such long shafts of words creating images, surrounded by wide spaces of emptiness, remarkably form an energetic resemblance, an invitation to the mysterious, direct experiences themselves.

And within this great mystery, every time another round of energy moves into me. I forget to recognize the signs that alert me to its arrival. I forget to ask for help. I forget to remember the last vision. And I forget still that I have known the gifts of high order, protection, and a profound innocence regarding the entire process. With each new invitation I recognize the suffering, the ecstasy, and once again surrender to the divine forces that be, to the infinite unknown. When it is over, I write, an old story retold anew. And once again I learn that my teacher is the energy itself, the visions, the emergence of a subtle, unmistakable clarity.

As though in labor before a child is born, I experience a knowing beneath the not knowing, beneath the dying of my old form, that I am a participant in transition from one world to another, embodying a passageway toward new life. As dawn breaks into this new day, the hot water of the bath holds me as I see *Arching Backward* released from the heat of the fire, the rest contained within me, secrets now forever.

|0| *Burned*
to white bone
I arch forward
curving down
through a void

burned into being
by the absence
of journals
no longer here.

Arching forward
down, the top
of my head
crowns
into and through
the center
of the fire.

In new life
forged
through flame
I make
my offering.

Looking through the glass doors, I see Theo coming down the hill with the dogs. I get out of the tub slowly because, as always, it is very hard to move after receiving a vision. I feel weak and enormously relieved. Pulling on my robe, I let the water out, put the soap dish back, lay the bath mat over the curved edge of this old tub, smoothing it with my hand. I take the candle with me through the door and back into the household where the white orchids in the center of the round table greet me, welcome me home. I am comforted by the candle light now as I fill the kettle, drop the tea leaves into the pot, and reach for two cups. I can see the doves safely held by the ivy twining. I can see one white lily, first opening of spring.

LYING DOWN

()

November 11, 1979
The Crew House

Longing to move, I have come to the studio above the boats. I see the pond through these windows that roll open, out toward and over the water. In here, the floor, walls, and ceiling are of dark wood placed in long, thin strips. Returning again to Authentic Movement, I return to the only vessel that can hold the complexities of my life. As long as I can move and be witnessed within the form of this discipline, I find a way through to a clearing.

I want a witness while I move here, another person to hold consciousness. But I do not want to talk about my experience of my movement and I do not want to hear about my witness's experience while I was moving. Rosa and I have been spending more and more time together. Recently in conversation we discovered that she wants a moving model at this time in her work as a visual artist. Since I need my witness to be silent, we try this collaborative approach for the first time today. Rosa sits to the side of the space, drawing as she witnesses me.

I step in. This space, open and empty, invites me. There are no other people in this space or nearby. There is no need to fill it. Moving through it, slowly, in such awe, it is hard to believe how clear, how free it is. This space is mine. Putting my cheek in my hand, I sink slowly toward the floor.

I lie down on my back, knees bent, feet flat. I feel warm, the grey wet of the morning surrounding me. I sink slowly into my body, receiving my weight, receiving myself. I am opening. An energy field appears between my legs, pushing them apart. The movement is infinitesimal, slow, until my legs fall open wide. With eyes closed, I see images.

◖◗ *My hands reach toward my yoni, pulling out a long, long rope, laden with lingams. Hand over hand I pull. Under the last lingam is a vibrant sphere, textured and beautiful. As it opens, a baby falls out. She glides back into me now,*

becoming a pubescent girl, released with utter joy and
freedom to explore my entire pelvic cavity. It is open in there,
pink and wet, free of organs. She moves, as if swimming, with
big and full strokes. She is home, returning home.

Opening my eyes, I return to Rosa. She offers me her drawing. I receive it silently, gratefully. We walk home together.

February 14, 1980
The Crew House

Rosa and I have been coming here once a week for the past three months. Each time, she sits to the side of the space, drawing while I move. Afterward we do not speak together of our experience. I always begin moving with the deep, slow pull downward and into the floor. Increasingly rich images appear in vivid detail. They are different from fantasies I have experienced in the past, the texture and light more vibrant. Over time, people, animals, places, and things begin to reappear in these images, weaving a story. Through confrontation with rage, fear, and loss, the pubescent girl has unfolded into the fullness of woman-hood, the process of developing consciousness embodied. As these grey, quiet mornings have evolved, the magnolia tree outside the windows behind Rosa has become winter bare, the light finding more space between branches as it filters into the studio.

This collaboration with Rosa feels vital, each of us fully into our own inner work. Today the studio is surrounded by white, snow vibrating on every surface. Rosa begins to draw. I lie down, knees bent, feet flat, clearly a process unfinished. Something new, small, and undulating curves upward, beginning in my lower back, up through my torso, neck, and head. This movement expands as I roll, my arms falling out and down. I feel desperate, reaching for something, knowing fully that I am nowhere near it.

April 28, 1980
The Crew House

It is late afternoon, a low, quiet day. Rosa and I walk here together. In the studio I find myself in the same starting position as always: on my back, knees bent, feet flat. My movement is unusually fluid, free, sensual and from a deep source. Again, with eyes closed, I see images.

◖◗ *A river runs fast and downward to my right. Reaching, I grab a duck floating by, bringing her to me. She walks into my mouth, looking down my throat. Discovering a silver ring around the inside of my throat, she pulls it out, placing it around my neck. Now I spin the ring in my lap as it pulls me away into the rushing river.*

June 14, 1980
The Crew House

Rosa sits in a slightly different place. I see the magnolia blossoms behind her, to her right. I lie down on my back, knees bent, feet flat. I close my eyes. Slowly my pelvis moves upward. I see images.

◖◗ *A man lifts hidden gems out of me, one by one, with his tongue. Each one blossoms, explodes, expands, becoming more. This is happening ever so slowly, so sensuously.*

May 30–June 4, 1981
Village Hill

A year has passed, a year of enormous challenge. The integration of my separation from Nathan has been completely demanding on all levels, deeply and constantly touching my experience of myself, my experience of others. Rosa and I met in the studio regularly through the year. She witnessed. I moved. I am so grateful for having what I needed—a place, a safe place, the right witness, and the discipline itself.

As the winter melted I saw ahead a bit. By next autumn, with both boys in school, there will be more time to practice, study, and teach Authentic Movement. I began preparations for the opening of a small institute where this could happen. The idea of returning more fully to the world and, more importantly, to my new questions within the discipline, is exciting.

Now there is time for another layer of this preparation, my own inner work. I have come to Rosalind's house for a seven-day retreat. I left David and Zachary slowly, ambivalently. They are going to the ocean with Nathan. It is harder to leave them since we have been separated. I love them each so far beyond any language that might say how much.

My room has been prepared. It is my favorite room in this house: the one with the wall of stones, the chair under the long horizontal window, the beige and blue quilt on the bed, the lantern with a candle that always burns me into sleep. I can walk in the forest, move in the Quonset hut, take long naps. Finally there is time and space to listen, time to be alone with my own inner rumblings.

Rosalind will be teaching dance at the college during the days but will be here in the evenings for long suppers by the fire. Tonight, eating eggs and oysters, we meander in conversation in a familiar way, beyond what we know toward questions that have no answers, toward freedom somehow. She tells me about her sons and her lovers. She tells me about this morning when she walked past the mirror in the hall by the front door. She turned to look again, seeing an old lady with white hair not falling softly into place, seeing for the first time a crone. She knows the dark intimately, having suffered too much, and yet it is as though her survival creates a unique radiance. She moves with a lightness that reflects her small frame. I recognize her aesthetics as I feast on the emptiness, the clarity, the striking beauty of her home.

As I prepare for bed, I remember dreams from this past year. They all are here with me, entries in my journal. Here is one: Mother takes her drawing and flings it into another season—autumn. Then in autumn: I say to two very tired young women, "You may not drive this bus. My children and I will be riding in it and you won't drive it safely." Another one: A beautician prepares to cut my hair. She sternly announces: "Bring the blindfold!" I challenge her, insisting that it is my hair and that I will see it being cut off.

In the winter, I wrote of this dream: I am walking in a heavy snow-storm, wearing my black cape. I move more and more slowly and get sleepier and sleepier. I fall to the ground and know that I am falling asleep. I realize I could die, frozen in the snow. And finally this last dream, still unsettling: The enemy occupies our community. My friends are nearby, frightened, crying. Everything is changing, even the language and the jobs are different. I cannot do this new dance. My steps are not sharp, quick, balanced. One foot is not joining this tight rhythmic shuffle. I am losing control over my own life.

Last night I slept deeply, the candle burning in the lamp all night. I awakened once and felt how dark it was, dark and still. It is noon now. I go to the Quonset hut. I move with no witness. I am entirely alone with my own experience, moving into another space within me, empty, untouched. How I long for this, how I fear it.

As I lie down, knees bent, feet flat, the sun emerges from the clouds, its light pouring into me. I feel starkly seen. I am the edge of a sharpness in bright light. It is painful. My arms slowly cross and block the light. The darkness, deeply soothing, is correct. Suddenly my arms fly open, straight out, my hands bending back at my wrists. The light shoots into me, hurting me. Back and forth—from being seen to utter darkness. I so prefer the dark, silent, inside place. So it is true. I am ready to go there, a place where no one can see me, shape me by their experience of me, a place where only I can see myself.

BURNING

()

July 30, 1981
Village Hill

I am here on Rosalind's land in the Quonset hut with David and
Zachary. We roast marshmallows on the fire in the center of the hut,
play games, and get into our sleeping bags, listening to the night
sounds. I dream in a deep color of purple, about Rosalind, about some
difficult work that has to be done. I awaken in the middle of the night.
I see images, now definitely not fantasies. I have no words to describe
this experience of seeing. Still more vivid in light and line, these images
brand me, marking me with fire.

[0] *I see myself*
completely still
my face solemn
long, classic.
My collarbone
burns
blue, small
flames
reaching, burning
my jawbone.

I see scar tissue
now covering
my jawbone
my collarbone.
My head tilted
up, I am touching
the burned place
gingerly.

8

August 17, 1981
Westport Beach

This feels like a new beginning. I have come to know a man named
Theo. Tall, blond, and bearded, I experience him as unusually centered.
He knows about the earth, about qualities of light, about song. He
seems not to be afraid of the ocean, of the sky, of seeing or being seen.

October 4, 1981
The White House

This time of year always feels potent. The boys are in school, though I
pick up Zachary at noon after a morning of kindergarten. I love walking
the few blocks among these big old houses and trees on the edge of the
college campus to bring him home. David walks home alone in the
afternoon, now that he is a third grader. When he arrived home today
he seemed so serene as he spoke about the sound of the rain falling on
his slicker.

The new students have finally arrived for a year of work at the Institute.
I wanted our first meeting to be elegant. We set a beautiful table in the
empty studio downstairs. The twins who live next door, their long blond
braids tied in pink velvet, served an exquisite gourmet dinner that Ada
prepared for us as a gift. Adele flew in from the West Coast, even
though she must fly back before finally living here and teaching the
weekly seminar. I wanted Lady Godiva chocolates for dessert. I wanted
beauty at every level. I wanted the women to feel welcomed, to somehow recognize each other, to be glad that they have risked committing
to this tiny new school that will be finding form in direct relationship to
the discipline of Authentic Movement finding form.

Today unfolds with an ease and a rhythm that is familiar. I feel nourished, light in weight, with a sense of mystery around me. Now at dusk, I lie down next to Theo, closing my eyes as I lay my head between his neck and shoulder, surrendering my weight.

◖◗ *I see me being pulled toward a tunnel. I enter the tunnel, the darkness. Becoming a yellow duck, I turn and begin to walk out. But now I turn again, away from the light, and pick up a silver ring that lies in a small pool of water.*

October 5, 1981
The White House

After the boys are in bed, I go into the small studio downstairs. Walking slowly in a spiral, circling downward, I feel an enormous weight on my back. Soon I can barely move, and finally fall over on the floor.

◖◗ *I see the duck leaving a cave. Coming toward me, she stops at a pool of water, picking up the silver ring. First she places it around Theo's neck. Then, as she takes it off, it becomes a long silver line with a hook on the end. Dipping it into Theo's throat, she pulls out gems, not yet polished, one by one, placing them in the center of the pool. The pile of these roughly shaped stones grows into a small volcano that erupts. New life appears at the top.*

October 29, 1981
The White House

The house, full of flowers, good food, and generous people, is quiet again. The public opening celebration for The Mary Starks Whitehouse

Institute is over. Earlier, as I was talking to the guests about the discipline of Authentic Movement and then introducing the featured speaker,
Clara, I felt quite strange and suddenly without an ease or comfort on
which I count when I am speaking in front of others. I thought maybe I
was becoming ill. Maybe I am ill. I cannot walk up the stairs to bed.
Theo helps me. We lie down. There is much pain in my lower back, and
I am barely able to move. With eyes closed, I see my students.

> **◖◗** *Eight women*
> *make a circle*
> *around me.*
> *I lie in the center.*
> *My whole body*
> *burns.*
> *The flames*
> *two inches high*
> *sear me*
> *silently.*
>
> *The pain is unbearable.*

October 30, 1981
The White House

It is early evening. I am acutely aware of the delicacy of the white
curtains on the bay windows across the room from us. I like reading to
the children here in my bed, one on each side of me. Rosa and
Lawrence come with supper. Lawrence makes a fire for me, a great gift.
Rosa takes the boys downstairs. Though Clara is packed and ready to
return to California tomorrow morning, she speaks of her reluctance to
leave me like this. Ada stops by to see me, asking many questions.
Adele arrives, sits on the bed , and we talk about the pain in my body
and these images of fire. There is so much vibration in my body, as if
another force or energy is filling me. After a deep but short sleep, I feel

almost completely immobile and can barely talk or keep my eyes open. Surrendering, I close them.

> **[()]** *I lie on my back*
> *my legs numb*
> *slowly disappearing.*
> *I have no lower half.*
>
> *I see*
> *a strong white light*
> *far away*
> *a dark source*
> *blinding*
> *shining, now softer*
> *now brilliant*
> *again.*
> *Ancient, huge*
> *structures emerge*
> *out of its shadow.*
>
> *My wrists are burning.*
>
> *I am standing*
> *my wrists sizzling*
> *my hands*
> *burning off*
> *floating in the air.*
> *My arms plunge*
> *into my pelvis*
> *burning*
> *two holes*
> *with my wrists.*
>
> *All tangled now*
> *I float and feel*

stuck, without a head
no hands.

I am burning.

I take these hands
burning
along the path
to the cave.
Theo
the ring, the pool
and the duck
welcome me, still.

Placing my hands
in the pool
lying face down
smoldering
the fire goes out.

The duck
lays eggs at the top
of my thighs.

November 1–3, 1981
High Meadow

Theo has brought us to his cottage on the farm in the Berkshires for the weekend. Before we left, I lay in bed feeling helpless and ashamed as he and Nancy gathered my things for the trip over the mountain. She held up a rose-colored blouse and asked if I thought I would need it. I didn't know. I don't know. I don't know what is happening to me.

There is more space now. We are closer to the earth and closer to the sky. I lie down in the loft here in the cottage. Theo has put yellow roses in a vase by the window and a pot of tea beside me. The tree outside the window is bare. Past the branches, I can see Theo and the boys near the barn feeding the horses in the twilight. I hope we brought Zachary's mittens. He doesn't have them on. Closing my eyes, reality shifts so quickly.

[O] *As though Theo asks*
I hear:
Do you feel hopeful?
Could your neck
become clear?
Will it open?

Opening
huge dark eyes
peer out
from within me.
A creature reaches
now leaps out
jumping
up and down, roaring
gnashing his teeth
and ripping open
the neck of a wolf.

Shoving
his hand down
into the body of the wolf
he pulls out a stone
white
spinning it
between
his thumb and forefinger.

Theo holds an egg
in both hands
one on top
the other on the bottom.
Seven birds
pastel in color
fly out
making a circle
around
the opening
of the wolf's neck.

The creature again
reaches down
into the body
of the wolf
pulling the tongue
hard
pulling it out
slicing it open
from front to back
placing
the white stone
inside.
Silver rings
slip around
holding it together.

The birds carry
the tongue
up to the moon
and into her mouth
now crowning her
with their bodies.

The moon
spits the tongue
out into the universe.
Falling
falling, landing
the tongue opens
revealing the white stone.
Falling
the white stone
opens, revealing
a diamond.

I offer it to one man.
He voraciously
swallows it.
I see it
traverse the path
through his guts.
I offer the diamond
to Theo.
Refusing
he places it
on the palm of his hand.
The diamond suspended
before me
he waits.

Taking it
in my right hand
I know
my first holding.

November 17, 1981
The White House

I need help badly. Friends have been trying to find someone to live with us to help with the cooking, the housekeeping, and when appropriate, with the children. Lila, a graceful young art student who seems to be a sensitive person, moved into the room on the third floor today. I have asked her to do the shopping, laundry, and cleaning so that I can use the energy I do have to be with the boys. She will also cook for me, since I am trying different and odd diets in an effort to soothe my stomach.

I find the small, pear-shaped diamond in the lockbox and take it to the jeweler. He will put it on a silver chain. I need to wear it, a talisman. I feel the burning in my back intensify each day, blue fire on a knife's edge. I see.

❍ *A woman in black*
the darkest black
slim, lithe
toes pointed
turns and turns
over and into a ball
falling
falling
into a raging
fire
becoming me.

My legs straddle
the fire.
The flames leap
above my head
all around me
shooting into my yoni

up and out
of my mouth
my hair burning
flying
behind me.

November 20, 1981
The White House

I am wearing the diamond. Lila brings me a beautiful tray for supper, poached pears and brown rice. Near the pale-pink napkin she has placed a white baby rose in the small vase from grandmother Woolf's house. Her aesthetics are lovely and make such a difference to me. Theo is downstairs wrestling with David and Zachary. They are laughing. I feel they are safe and happy. Now I can surrender to the pressure behind my eyes as I move from this world to another.

[○] *The entire inside*
of my body
burned to nothing
the inside of my skin
empty and black
I lie on my back
legs up, knees bent.

With a knife
in my right hand
I cut
from my yoni
upward to the base
of my throat.
I cut off my arms
at my elbows

at my shoulders.
I cut
at my knees
at my thighs.
I place the lips
of my yoni
at the base
of my throat
inside.

A flying fish
its mouth flecked
in gold, sails
through the lips.
Struggling, she lands
gliding
under some stones.

A lingam burns
against the lips
seeking entrance.

Wide open
I lie on my back
legs up, knees bent.
Women, exotic
five or seven
dark-skinned
hair wrapped
on the top of their heads
tug
on a white rope
stepping backward.

The other end
lies
between my legs.

Blood pours
out of my yoni
into the sand
forming a river
flowing away from
me.

The women dance
around me
leaping over
the river of blood
covering their bodies
covering my body
with my blood
with my blood.

More come
placing their heads
on top of my pubis
tumbling on over
somersaulting
and slipping
into the river of blood.

[O] *I am straddling*
a pit
swollen with black liquid.
A great black monster
roars out of it
pushing inside me
eating me, tearing me
part by part.

Biting, ripping
the parts fall

into the cauldron
burning and burning
in the fire
of the pit.
Dark men dance
around the burning
black liquid.

A simple
stone structure
appears over the pit
made of hundreds
of smooth round stones.
The dancers
dance round it
and through it.
The structures
become many.
The dancers become more.
The dancers dance
around the stone structures.
The structures stand
over black burning pits.

November 21, 1981
The White House

[0] *People, ancient people*
from a very old city
quietly mill
around the structures
of stone.

There are horses
more people
waiting
for a person.
I remember I know her
a leader
to come.

I feel frightened
so frightened.

I stop seeing.

February 12, 1982
The White House

My sleep for days has been deep and unsettling. I cannot digest food. Before a nap, I see.

[0] *I am being pulled*
intensely, slowly
without relief
forward
by a force.
I am a small
red-hot arc.

UNRAVELING

【】

March 26–29, 1982
High Meadow

I know now that these images are visions. Adele has helped me to
understand this, and my own experience makes it clear. This energy,
which burns through my bones, my cells, directly and deeply affecting
my entire body, also somehow creates pictures. These images are made
of light, of an electric vibration. The clarity of line, form, and depth
reflects a reality beyond fantasy, dream, or ordinary perception.

I also know that I am in a process. I perceive an order, a direction, even
a rhythm, though the impact of each vision on my body, my awareness,
is so great that there is no space yet for understanding or even sensing a
context for all of this. Each vision expands the universe, changing my
perception, changing then, my experience of myself. Though my life is
becoming extremely complex and difficult, I do feel deep gratitude. I am
receiving a gift. I remember the words of John Weir in Bethel: "The only
way out is in and through." I do not know what else to do.

It is spring vacation and Lila has a break. I am not sure she is the right
person for this job. She often seems overwhelmed with our situation, as
such a young woman might well be. The boys are with Nathan. I worry
about them sensing these changes in my body. Though sometimes I
move slowly, I never actually see visions when they are with me. I wait
to let the energy through when they are sleeping, at school, with
Nathan, or at a friend's house.

I have been trying to hold back the energy as it builds, until now, when
there is time here with Theo, to receive it. The pressure behind my eyes
increases, the fire in my back intensifies, and all movement slows down.
Sleep and digestion are constantly interrupted. I am learning that these
sensations all are signs that I must prepare for a retreat. Finally I am
able to make space.

In the loft, in bed, I surrender to a kind of exhaustion I have never felt
before. The burning and aching, the weeping, and the strange deep

24

sleeping are relentless. How will I be able to continue to teach? Theo paints at his easel near the window. The violet he is using attracts me, the curved lines satisfying. The change in direction comes easily today as I shift from what I see around me to what I see within.

[()] *I see*
a sliver of red light
glowing
on the faraway edge
of a mountain range
at noon.

The mountains
slowly slip into
a lake, water
swelling, creating
an ocean.

I lie quivering
on the inside
of an immense white
wave
resisting
the pull under.

[()] *An Old Woman, dark*
Native American
shoos the children
out of my room.
Turning
in her cape
she closes the door.

Opening
the top button
of my gown

she licks
the upper left
side of my sternum
where the second or third
rib
meets the flat bone.

She washes my body
scraping away
the white soap
leaving the scraper
of long wood
between my thighs.

A circle of dark men
naked and dancing
circle around me.

I awaken
leaning on the wood
standing
in the center
of the men fiercely dancing
dressing me
in long heavy robes
crowning me
with feathers of owls.

Bedecked in jewels
I am lifted
onto a black horse
and start turning.
The saddle is spinning.
The people dance
wildly.

I spin
off of the saddle
and back down

on the horse
violently sucked
into a black hole.

The earth buries us.

Barreling out
of the earth
on the horse
these robes, this crown
my shining gems
slip away
one by one
until
I am naked.

Now I lie down
in the grass.
A giant fist
pounds my right eye
in slow motion
opening
my head, my body.
Insects are hammering
gnawing and crawling
until my bare skeleton
shatters into bones
broken and splintered.

I cry as I watch.

[○] *Two feminine*
white hands
touching
at the base of the palms
reach into a small circle
of blood

at a spot midway
on my spine.
These hands
open, as fingers
catch a silk thread
winding
my whole body
with the scarlet
thin strand.

My body tied
bound, lies long
in an ancient
earth-red
sheath of clay.
Days pass.

Theo carries me
unraveling
limp
on my back
across his arms.
Seven women follow
into the forest
where the Old Woman
sits waiting.

He lays me
in her lap
her skirts filling
with water, a whirlpool
of wetness
swirling around me.

Spitting
five times
on my neck
down my sternum

she licks
up and down
my white, flat bone.
Placing her mouth
deep into mine
she spits into the back
of my throat.

A long black snake
rides on her spittle
into my right arm
out my hand.
The snake sews me
together
sticking its tongue
through the bone
of my pubis
my right foot
my left foot
now piercing
my wrists.

I am sewn, hung
like a hammock
from the tree
dangling above
the Old Woman
who listens.

The tree rocks me
now drops me.
Theo and the Old Woman
catch me together
as my skin
peels off
layer after layer
my energy mounting.

The seven women
press against
Theo and the Old Woman
who hold me
more tightly
while I become
once again
sheathed in
the shape of the mummy.

A woman near
my Old Woman
my dark Old Woman
tries to unravel
the scarves
that tie me
bind me there.
But the dark one
says no.

The women sit
in a wide circle
witnessing.
The Old Woman ties
pieces of my skeleton
broken
splintered and cracked
with black thread
hanging them
from the tree
so they burn
from the fire
in the center below.

An ephemeral white figure
lifts

UNRAVELING

my burning bones
wrapped in white muslin
into the sky
guarding them
kicking
to propel herself
higher.

She with my burning
bones
swims
through dark tunnels
of clouds, dives
into the mouth
of the moon, down
her throat
deeply down
through yet darker tunnels
and lays
my black burning
bones in a box
on a wheel.

The wheel spins
slowly, now faster
and faster, creating
a force that splits
white stone.
Fragments fall away
revealing
a dark-skinned
woman.

I do not know her.

April 1, 1982
The White House

It is late into the night. These visions, and many I cannot record, continue to bombard me for hours, all night, tumbling on top of each other. They are brutal. I must sit up. I cannot lie down, even for a second, because I cannot risk surrendering my capacity to witness myself. There is less separation between me-in-the-visions and me. I *know* I must not merge with the images. If I should merge, I would risk losing my relationship to them. It is the relationship that sustains my consciousness and my hope of eventually integrating this material. I know this from my years of work as a therapist. Merging with the material, identifying with it, can surely create psychosis.

The visions keep repeating themselves as I become more and more frightened, on the edge of and sometimes immersed in real panic. Lila stays with me until Theo arrives. My body aches and burns beyond description. I am too afraid.

> **◖◗** *A hooded man*
> *in black*
> *chops me into pieces*
> *always starting*
>
> *at my feet.*
> *Now, lifting his hood*
> *sensitive, loving*
> *he takes me under*
> *beautiful, clear water.*
>
> *A giant fist*
> *smashes*
> *an infant's face*
> *into infinity.*
>
> *A giant fist*
> *gripping an ice pick*

plunges
into each of my eyes.

A giant fist
gripping an ice pick
pierces
the palms of my hands.
I hang crucified.

The pick
drives through my ankles
not holding
ripping my skin
endlessly.

An immense wheel
in space
spins.
An animal with claws
tries desperately
to hold on
to climb up
elongating its body.

Terrifying, terrified
I become the animal
slipping, falling
into infinity.

An axe slices
a woman's body
in half.
I see her bones
impeccably describing
her form.

Great, black insects
crawl

out of her body
toward my face.

Relieved
I float in the black
river of the dead.
Corpses
surround me.

I surrender.

April 2, 1982
The White House

Nathan arrives with a basket of oranges and great plans for an adventure with David and Zachary. We speak together for a while about the children and about my health. He offers to help by being with the boys more often. As he and the children leave, I am aware of allowing myself to stop resisting the energy so much. When the children are here, which is most of the time, I try very hard to be present with them, keeping the energy at bay. It is becoming a rigorous discipline, trying to balance the force of the energy and my deep ambivalence in relationship to it with my great desire to mother my boys well and consistently. This ambivalence is tricky. The energy is saving my life in some indescribable way and simultaneously, it is taking my life.

Theo comes to get me. He carries me upstairs and while he packs my clothes, he tells me more about Diana, an especially sensitive chiropractor. He has made an appointment for me as we agreed he would. We stop on our way to High Meadow to see her. She uses the word emergency in speaking about my adrenal glands and my immune system. She says I must stop working immediately and radically change my diet. I ask about my heart and its unsettling beats and rhythm. She says I am experiencing something called coronary reflex. Everything she says confirms what my body tells me, yet I cannot imagine rearranging or ending my teaching commitments.

April 6, 1982
The White House

I am exhausted. It takes constant work to vigilantly maintain the boundary between the visions and my ego-consciousness. I feel desperately weak, unable to sleep, and less and less able to ward off the darkness. Diana is right. I know I cannot continue with the Institute. I simply do not have enough energy to responsibly care for the children, correctly prepare to see visions, see them, rest and recover from each round, and be faithful to my teaching and planning for each student. I lie down here in my room and close my eyes.

[O] *Theo looks into*
the fire, gently
opening it
with his hands
revealing
at the bottom
a tiny, white creature.
Picking it up
cradling it
in his arms, it dives
between the buttons
inside his sweater
a shape
no face, no fingers
with the tail
of a fish.

Theo strolls
in the forest
carrying this being
his face upward
as he walks.

He is singing.

April 8, 1982
High Meadow

[0] *I see*
each day
a long and thin
wooden boat.
Within two dark red
barrels
stand on each side
of a slim
dark figure.

The boat waits
in the water
on this side
of a black, iron
latticed gate.

An ominous being
looms
on the other side
of the unmovable gate.

The task:
lift the gate
pass by the threatening
being
move the boat
through a narrow
waterway
and out into the sea.

I see each day
the boat waiting
the man
waiting.

Wanting the gate
to open
I try
and I fail.

I wait.
Today
the gate lifts
a heavy cloth
covers, diminishes
the menacing force
the boat moves through
and the slim figure
dives
into the sea
free.

There is within me a new sensation, a delicate, yet constant vibration. I can almost hear it. The pit of my stomach is opening for breath. I sense a silver-blue lining all around the new space. I am drinking air. Throughout the day I feel deep pleasure when my body reminds me that I can breathe all the way down. This is the first concrete gift from this journey. I can breathe.

April 11, 1982
High Meadow

[()] *I see a great hole*
above me.
Fire blasts out
in bullets
igniting me.

Now I am the fire.
I burn others.

This is unbearable.

No. This cannot be so. This is too painful. Burning others is worse than being burned.

April 16, 1982
Village Hill

I have come to Rosalind's for the afternoon, after a week that was extremely hard. Theo found Lila crying at the top of the back steps. She told him that my experiences and needs are not too much for her, but the management of the household on top of that is overwhelming. It is all so much more than her original image of watering the plants, reading fairy tales to the children, and bringing me trays of delicate foods. She cannot stay. I understand completely. What will we do?

Sleeping is so difficult. There is too much quick vibration in my heart that radiates throughout my body, especially when I awaken. I must close the Institute. I cannot teach. I need to correctly complete this commitment to my students now, so that I can finally retreat into the solitude for which I long. There is much to be done—work with Adele in planning for my withdrawal, work with each individual student and with the group as a whole toward closure, and of course, work with the finances. Just thinking about it all is overwhelming and painful. I cannot bear my inability to meet my own expectations and those of my students. I lie down by the fire.

> **◖◗** *I see*
> *a scrawny black bird*
> *with crooked feathers*

UNRAVELING

a long neck
a long skinny bill.
He lies on his back
his enormous mouth
open.

A feminine force
places pearls
translucent, white eggs
in the gaping
dark cavern.
Rising, now diving
he buries one
at the bottom of the sea.

Digging, retrieving
the pearl
in his mouth
tied to silk thread
he surfaces
shooting straight
and long into the sky.

Returning
he writes in the sand
with the pearl
as his pen:
Sojern Pleuribus
Rottellme.

◖◗ I see a dark woman
mute
in a long, black gown.
Many roots stretch
out from her feet.

Her arms, her hands
open to hold.

A tree floating
in the night universe
she is sucked
gently into the mouth
of a great white mist
dragon in shape.

Her roots
too cumbersome
she remains there
in his mouth
still now
not fitting.

My arms, my upper torso are completely clear, empty of matter, but there is such active, alive energy vibrating inside the outer shape. This is an extraordinary sensation.

(0) *I see front steps*
swept clean
one bush, nearby
ready to bloom
the ground raked
a clearing.

(0) *I see fire orange*
sparkling
crinkling spheres
popping
out of the center

of the white shape
Theo found
at the base of the fire.

White feminine hands
rescue one.
It falls away
breaking open
on the ground
revealing a filament
maybe a flower
white
erect
and alive.

April 21, 1982
The White House

Today the Institute closes, two months early. Letting go of this responsibility and commitment is excruciating. I feel incredibly impatient with myself and can think only of my mistakes. I place the clay sculptures I made for each one of my students in a circle in the small studio downstairs, awaiting their arrival. Each piece is formed by my experience as a witness of their movement. It is a painful session. Some seem to understand, some, especially Anna, are angry. Some feel abandoned. Sophie reaches across the circle and hands me a pearl from her grandmother's necklace that rests in a tiny blue velvet pouch. With compassion, she wishes me well on my journey.

I lie in the small studio downstairs, under the bay window, after the women leave. Deeply relieved and terribly afraid, I see into the empty space.

[O] *A great dark*
and frightening figure
scoops me
up with his slick
black hands.
I am so small
on my back
rigid and white.

He eats me.

[O] *Anna moves*
with abandon.
Moving
she finds a splinter
really, a thorn
cone-shaped
in her tongue.

She comes to me
her witness
taking the thorn out
of her tongue
pouring the blood
collected in its shape
into a small crevice.

The crevice of smooth wood
on top of a knot
in a small tree
stands between us.
At the knot
two different branches
grow up and out.

Between them
it is empty.

EMPTYING
【】

April 23-27, 1982
High Meadow

I have taken the children out of school for a week. Returning to High Meadow with them brings profound relief. The trees seem like spirit creatures welcoming me, the stream is gushing silver, the wind light and warm. I feel as though I am in a stupor. This energy is destroying my body. My mind is crystal clear, but my body is dying.

I can stop at any moment in the midst of receiving a vision if David or Zachary awaken or suddenly arrive home early. In that way I am not in a trance. I can prepare food also, though my own hunger in such a state is minimal. During the times when I am not receiving many visions, I try to attend to our daily lives—relationships, grocery shopping, or the arrangement of our schedules. I drive as little as possible. When I am here with Theo, he takes care of so much of that. And he keeps reminding me to listen to my exhaustion and my aching stomach. I am so deeply focused on learning how to just manage this energy, I do not remember to take time to learn how to care for my body.

Today Adrianne and her boys come from New York. Their visits are so important for all of us. She is like a sister to me. I need to talk with her. And Changa has puppies today. All day long she births her puppies—new life appearing, one by one, until there are eight, two not living, too far from the opening, not enough air. The children are completely engaged. I am completely engaged. Midwifing grounds me. Reaching into the birth canal with my hand, searching for those not yet born, I am at home.

Theo and I go to bed late. Lying down in the loft, I become immobilized. Suddenly turning my head to the left, my neck feels painfully exposed.

> **[O]** *Slice.*
> *My neck*
> *opens.*
> *I see inside*

the small
wooden crevice
holding the thorn
full of blood
and the diamond.

My neck
now closes
fastened shut
with a loop
and a button.

(0) *I see the red light*
tumbling
down the mountain
floating in the ocean.
Slowly
a large grey rock
rises up
out of the water
in two halves
a giant vulva
swallowing the light.

The light
now inside
this great rock
inside the ocean
inside me
still shines.

(0) *I see*
a great white bird
white head

white wings
tipped in color
standing at the edge
of a clearing
in the forest.

People come
in stillness
insect size
unafraid
to be near this
calm, peaceful bird.

I see inside
the grey rock
in the ocean.
The red light
on a stick
becomes a skeleton
of a bird
flapping
half-alive
longing to break out
of the stone.

My insides flutter.

I bathe and wash my hair and lie in the sun for a long time. After breakfast on the porch, as I get up, I feel my body coming back. In the late afternoon, Theo and I walk to the meadow with the boys to see the horses. The air is soft. The light shifts magnificently. Back in the loft, when night arrives, I lie down.

Now tiny people
crawl

all over the great bird
stroking it
patting it gently.
I am one
of these people
deeply peaceful
caressing the bird.

The bird shoots
up into the blue.
Some try to hold on
but they fall
falling
back to earth.

It is night on the land where Theo begins to build the new house. We decide to sleep here. This is just what I need—to sleep directly on the earth. While he is gone getting our sleeping bags, I feed the fire, my gaze riveted upward. I bang on the stones with a stick, as though I am sacrificing myself to the gods and I want them to notice. I feel so small.

◖◗ *I see*
a cavern
in the earth
the walls
black mountains.

We are at the top
the great bird and I
hovering
over this cavity.
At the bottom
of the hollow
in the earth
tiny people
stand

by their fire
looking up
straight up
following the smoke.

The smoke
brushes the belly
of the bird
now brushes my legs
hanging down, over
the softness.
It is dark and night
down there.

We are in the light.

[O] *I see me*
in my cranberry
scoop-necked
sweater
my hair down.

I am walking
toward me
my eyes shining
purple light.
Stumbling
my arms lift
upward, balancing.
The visions
the sharp white light
interfere
with my seeing.

I am terrified
the me losing my sight
the me witnessing.

EMPTYING

[O] *In a cave*
I lie in a pool
of water. Tiny
half in the water
half out
I play idly
with the silver ring.

Now restless, I
suddenly turn over
beating
on the floor of the cave.
The earth cracks
opening.
I spit down
into the black nothing
three times
five times
seven times.

The crack
begins to close
my head caught inside.
I fight not to fall
into the abyss.
Now falling
dropping into the black
I land
on the back
of the great white bird.

We strike
straight out of emptiness
like a bullet
breaking through
the crust of the earth

up, into the light
of the sky.

Now I have a ride
thrilling and fast
slow and weaving
up
down, hugging
the softness
hugging and holding
my great white bird.

Standing
I fling my arms
into the soul
of the wind
blowing through me
fantastic, free.

Reckless, we fly
into the sun.
The great white bird
comes through
burned
its tail on fire.

I put out the fire.

Forest animals lick
my neck.
Cut open
and in the center
a man's hand appears
red, undulating
in slow motion
beckoning
wanting to pull in

the little animals
by their claws.

The animals refuse.

Now a pulsing fist
each time closing
birthing diamonds
the hand offers
these gems, one by one
to the creatures.
An old bell
behind the hand
rings
at the base of my throat.

My neck closes.
The animals
return to the forest
each
with her diamond.

Now in flight
once again
I straddle the bird
the great white bird
holding leather reins
in my hands.
In utter abandonment
I cross the reins
and pull.
Slicing through
the bird's neck
they cut it loose.
I am aghast.
Look what I have done!

The bird lands
in a great and green
summer tree.
The forest animals
toss their diamonds
into the center
of its.neck.

I lick and lick
the place
that is severed
full round.
The animals
help me, licking.
I lie down on the bird
waiting. I am waiting.

The great white bird
suddenly sits
up, flutters
its wings, flies away.
Left in the nest
feeling
afraid and helpless
I am full of shame.

Seven smooth
white birds
guard me
standing on the edge
of the nest, facing out.

The great white bird
comes to me
dropping seven tears
into my yoni

flying away
again.

Now all of me is spilling
water.
My whole body
weeps.
Water flows
out of every pore.

The white birds
come and drink.
I lie surrendered
in a stream, emptying.

Parts of my body
split off one by one
floating away
dissolving.

Seven dark people
appear, gathering
my fragments
lifting all of me
placing me
in a slot
in an oven
in the side of the earth.

The seven people
I think they are men
stomp in a circle
dancing
in the stream
in the weeping stream.

May 1-3, 1982
High Meadow

I feel impatient, weary of it all. My body aches and burns so. I cannot yet learn what or how to eat to alleviate my constant stomachache. After two days of desperate restlessness and terror, pressure behind my eyes and fire in my back, I feel the vision energy mounting but can see *nothing*. This is the worst. Finally, to my profound relief, form appears.

> **[0]** *I lie in the stream*
> *weeping, terrified*
> *the stream of my tears.*
> *I have seen me*
> *here for centuries*
> *the etched black line*
> *running*
> *from my pubic bone*
> *up to my throat*
> *the muscles themselves*
> *creating a meridian.*
> *Water pours*
> *especially from this line.*

Crying, I hold the bottom arches of my rib cage, two halves of a great rock. I feel frantic, terrified, as I writhe in pain. I cannot contain this alone. Theo comes back for lunch and hears me. He holds me. He licks my neck. I sleep. Awake again, I see.

> **[0]** *I am in the stream*
> *my body*
> *weeping, melting.*
> *I see the great*
> *sweet, white bird*
> *its head falling off*

revealing inside
a black head.

Now the white chest
opens
and the black bird
skinny and sprawling
walks out.
Transforming, becoming
full and healthy
he comes to me
in the water
and warmly
lies next to me.

Time passes.
They take the body
my body
out of the slit
in the earth.
I am Anna
totally burned
a white crumbling mass.

Lying next to me
face down
in the stream
Anna is Pride.
I stab her
shoving her off the cliff
to my right.
She falls
clutching the edge.
Guilt suggests
I save her. Trying
I fall
into oblivion.

I lie in the stream
tracing the meridian line
on my body
with my hands
a path carved
between the mountains
my rib cage
on both sides.

My head rolls
from side to side
drawing an arc
before me
a bridge
over the stream.

Dead people
I have loved
reach down
their long white arms
grabbing me
paralyzing
my neck.

I am dying. I scream for Theo in the barn, but the wind outside the
open window is wild and carries my voice away.

[O] *I see Theo*
on the bridge
leaning on a wooden railing
talking to me
as if he were really here.
I beg him to come.
He says no.

EMPTYING

I must see this one
alone.

Every time
I scream for him
he reassures me
he is here
but on the bridge.
Shoving away
the dead people
with a brush backward
of his strong, left hand
leaning over
he pours a little water
down onto me.
I am so thirsty.
Reaching down
he empties my body
of all matter.

My neck is now almost completely paralyzed. I am at the peak of my
terror. Suddenly I feel my hands, right over left, lying on the place
where the Old Woman licked me, near my sternum, on the second or
third rib, the place Adele calls the high heart. I feel a little thump under
my hands. Great energy fills my hands, the insides of my arms and
upper chest, my neck. The sensation is like my experience of the vision
last month when I saw the front steps swept clean. It is a moving,
sounding sensation.

Since the first vision my heart has been beating down, way down in my
solar plexus. I have not liked the sensation at all. It always awakens me
at dawn. Now I realize that this new energy has just found its way to
my high heart. I listen and receive it fully. This is bliss. My new heart is
pumping little bursts of life under my hands, upward, like buds bursting

into flowers. Today my heart has made the journey to a new home. I so hope it stays.

When Theo comes in, he holds me for a long time. He carries me downstairs and out onto the porch, into the soft light of late afternoon. He sings to me. I see the puppies crawling on their bellies in the grass nearby. I am alive.

PIERCED

【】

June 6–10, 1982
Jacob's Pillow

Until now, each vision has demanded all of my energy to such an extent that movement has been minimal while I actually receive the visions. Often I cannot open my mouth or my eyes. I lie so still and yet experience such intense activity within.

David and Zachary are with Adrianne and Sid in New York, a favorite place for them to be. Theo is only twenty minutes away at High Meadow and will come for me in five days. In the cool emptiness of this studio, many of us who studied with Mary Whitehouse gather to practice Authentic Movement together. Clara and I have been planning this conference for months, with me not knowing from week to week whether I would be able to attend. I have tried to rest as much as possible since the last round of visions. I decided to come at the last minute. I had to come. I trust my colleagues and Rosalind is here.

As one of the movers, I am aware of the two witnesses. I am dancing now as I have never danced before. I feel possessed. The vision force is moving me rather than keeping me from moving. Standing with knees bent, feet flat on the floor, my right heel goes up and down rhythmically. My legs are spread; all of my weight is in my pelvis. Now this energy that has been dominating my life for almost a year is truly moving me, entering through my heel. I am taken by the fury of its beat. Blazing upward, my head and arms are pulled up and out. The energy released, I lie down and close my eyes.

> **[0]** *A flash of light*
> *and I am looking*
> *down a deep*
> *narrow corridor*
> *with walls of gold.*
>
> *At the very end*
> *I see an old woman*
> *holding her dead son*
> *on her lap*

Rosalind and Bill
Mary and Jesus.
The son moves
toward me
in a prone position
feet, the large soles, first.
He needs food.

He is given bread.

Sickly, white
I see him
becoming a large bird
now transformed
a great, magnificent
swan
in a European park
floating on a pond
calm, familiar
more regal.

I am in the water
near him
wanting to touch
climbing over his back
quickly getting off.

I should not touch him.

I stand in the pond
waist high
like a child
gently splashing water
on his left wing.

The swan takes flight
taking my breath away
flying up
over my body
pushing me

underwater
my arms reaching up
to him.

He leaves me.

In the studio, preparing to move again, I take off my diamond, asking
Clara to hold it. I begin bent over, hands clasped in front of my sternum, scooting my feet along. A finger is touching me on the small of
my back. I wonder if it is Rosalind. Slowly I turn my head to the left,
turning my torso that way, trying to hear what this senior woman is
going to tell me. I sense that I am not allowed to face her. I keep
turning, ever so slowly. Then I realize that she is turning too, and
therefore is always behind me, her hands gently on my hips. Our arms
go out to the side, hers under mine. She is teaching me how to work
my wings. A long time passes. I try it on my own and soon I am
dancing, my heels pounding, my wings flapping.

◖◗ *Flying*
I am the swan
in the heavens
large and looking
down on the earth
for myself, the child
Jan
left behind in the pond.

Ecstatic, in flight
I am spinning
free.

As I leave the studio, I suddenly am afraid I have lost my diamond. I
haven't. Clara still has it. I take it to my room and somehow, within
seconds, lose it. There is a frantic search, many helping. We find it in my
sandal. After putting it on and checking the safety clasp several times, I
shower and dress for dinner in a summer white dress. In the car with
Clara and Rosalind, on our way to the restaurant, I check the clasp and

find again that it is open. Clara secures it once more. At the restaurant, we choose to eat in the garden. Just as I finish dinner, I panic as I realize the diamond is again gone. Looking down I see that it is held by my clothing, resting over the place where my second or third rib attaches to my sternum, the place where the Old Woman licked me, the place where my new heart landed. I see a tiny and perfect circle of blood under it with a hole in the middle. I have been pierced by the diamond.

In the studio the next day, after witnessing for a long time, I prepare to move again. I am dancing and I am too hot. I pull my purple turtleneck collar down toward my chest. I thrust my neck out, exposing it upward. My heels are beating the floor. Dancing this way for a long time, terrified, I come with full energy to a very specific sensation. I offer myself— to be sacrificed? In terror, I retreat. Again thrusting my neck out, pulling down harder on my collar, the particular sensation reccurs. I know I must offer my neck. More terror, then gradually I feel empowered.

I want to touch my neck—to protect it maybe—and know I am not allowed. Nothing is allowed to touch my neck. Suddenly and accidentally my collar touches my neck. Gasping, I fall to the ground with my fists jabbing into my pubic bone, screaming and rolling. Possessed, I collapse and am held by Rosalind. Sacrificed, I have embodied the pierce of the diamond.

Today I lie down in the corner of the studio, needing to be in a certain relationship to the two walls.

(0) *Cutting me open*
from pubic bone to throat
six men, black
empty my body
of all matter
using their hands
to scoop.

Now lifting me
tilting me
backward, on a slant

my warm blood
pours
into a leather hammock
slung
over a small fire.

The hammock, attached
to sticks
on either side of the fire
by leather loops
rocks, rocks
from side to side
the blood spilling
onto the fire
putting it out.

Leaping up
landing on my feet
bedecked in full costume
I am a deer
dancing
down the center
between two lines
of black men.

It is the last day of this gathering and I feel too tired. In these last months, I have lost fifteen pounds and am unusually frail. It is increasingly hard to come back from these experiences. I kneel in the upper left corner of the studio.

[O] *A very old woman*
Native American
I see far
down
into the valley
far up
into the sky.

STAYING OPEN

()

June 22, 1982
The White House

(I) *Running*
running terrified
I am smacked
in three places
the inside
of each ankle
and the nape
of my neck.
Signs
rosy pink
rise into
shape.

Marked by the spirits
I am an initiate.

July 4–7, 1982
High Meadow

David and Zachary are with Mother and Dad for a week at our house. I thought it would be less interruptive for them to be at home with all of their toys, with Changa, with everything familiar. David has an important baseball game coming up and this way he will not miss it. Rosa and Lawrence can help with Zach.

Today is too hard. It is a rainy, cold morning. I feel very shaky. My heartbeats are so unsettling. Theo and his friends help me here. Angela listens. She seems to understand. Since Jacob's Pillow my heel wants so badly to drum, but when it does I feel too afraid. Finally I lie down, all of me vibrating. My right hand somehow lands on my diamond wound.

My left hand covers my mouth. Now my right hand moves to touch my third eye. I feel calmer. It is as if the energy route has been marked.

I am deeply in what we now refer to as my "slows." I move very, very slowly, feeling great weight in my body and feeling at the same time suspended. As the day progresses I move more and more slowly. At the market I feel as though I am a different species from the other people around me. I drive home but I cannot get out of the car and stay there for an hour until Theo finds me. My mind is completely clear. My body will not always move.

Two days have passed in which I feel very slow and very strange. Hannah comes to visit. People often comment on how much we look alike. We do have similar coloring and the same bone structure. With some intuitive knowledge about all of this, she accepts the complexities of this process. Her humor is invaluable, her love of the boys ever-present. Because of her involvement with the Institute, she helps me sort through my pain around ending early last spring and my confusion in hoping to begin again in the autumn.

I do nothing of real value. The mistakes I have made so far in my life seem unbearable. I cannot tolerate my feeling of transparency in the presence of almost anyone. I cannot bear my self-consciousness, my shame. Seth, Theo's oldest and closest friend, is here and I am so uncomfortable not knowing how to explain. He is dear and nonintrusive. Walking outside, off the path and into the woods, I find a small plant that is uprooted, dead. Taking it inside, I decide to draw the roots in ink. It is satisfying to focus on the part of the plant that holds on underground.

Now the energy is fully within me but I cannot see images. No matter how terrible the visions are in content, they are a relief compared to this raw energy that finds no form. I am terrified and frantic. Theo brings me red clay. He makes a winged woman. I make a half-mask with two deep-set eyes, a beak for a nose, and a raised round where the third eye is. I feel slightly relieved and know I must get into a hot bath. Theo is with me. Now I am more frightened than I have ever been. This energy could kill me with its intensity, its force. I know my forehead has to be washed in preparation for wounding. I am too afraid and sobbing.

(0) *The Old Woman enters.*

My hands, palms down, are turned out at the wrists.

(0) *Wings grow*
white.

They flap, trying to scoop water to bring to my forehead. My feet move steadily, constantly.

(0) *I am a water bird*
paddling, preparing
for the wound.

My hands, horribly awkward, keep pulling at the center of my forehead, pulling the skin out in all directions, holding it open. Terror, complete terror, seizes me. I manage to put water there and keep trying to hold it open. Now my hands form a beak shape, my thumbs locking inside my upper teeth, fingers together, half on each side of my nose—a bill. As this happens, I lean far forward, my neck stretching wide, making deep primal sounds, deep and long groans.

(0) *Opening, elongating*
I sound
from my source.
I am a swan.

Twice the stab
comes to open
my third eye
first an ice pick
now a knife.

Blood runs
in a small river
down my face.
I cannot breathe.

Life stops.

Theo pours cold water from a small glass over my third eye. I feel his palm touching my forehead as he tips the glass. I am calmer. My forehead feels swollen and smooth. As he tries to give me water to drink, my hands work to hold my lips open. I cannot drink out of a glass. Theo's forehead touches mine for a long time. I feel needles of energy shooting between us. He pours cool water over this meeting place.

(0) *My wings slowly*
flap. Theo wrapped
around my belly
we journey
high
so high
I can barely
see the earth.

We are both exhausted yet feel drawn outside. Theo carries me out into the twilight, between the sinking sun and the rising moon. We lie in the grass under the pine tree, near the big rock, in silence. When it is completely dark, he carries me back inside to the loft. We talk about what I should do. It is all too much. He suggests I spend more time with the animals, finding allies.

(0) *I see two black*
half-moons
facing each other
trying not to close
the circle.

69

Words tell me:
Never let the wound
close completely.
It must always
stay open.

August 12, 1982
The White House

[0] *Cell by cell*
I turn
into a rabbit.
The change
absolutely excruciating
in my bones
in my tissue
occurs silently
the ears forgotten.

Now I have ears.

October 7–9, 1982
The White House

Theo and I took the boys to Westport Beach at the end of the summer, a special time. Playing on the dunes, cooking around the fire, making music, and swimming in the waves—I felt reassured and safe. Eating without stomach pain continued to be a challenge. We talked with the children, as we do from time to time, about my experience of this energy. I told them that, though it is often hard to receive, it is a gift. I told them that it makes me very tired but that it brings me into direct experience of the mysteries of the universe. It seems most impressive to them that I cannot watch movies or go to the summer carnival.

The summer is over and I have decided to try and teach again at the Institute. Adele will offer her weekly seminar, but it continues to be my responsibility to cover the rest of the work, in the studio and in seminars.

The new students have arrived. Like last year, they are either artists or newly trained therapists coming for post-graduate study. As I begin my teaching schedule again I realize I must find someone to live with us, someone who can help. I have to be able to teach through the academic year this time. Today I notice that the energy is coming back, but I cannot believe that it might continue. I feel exhausted just at the thought of such disruption, pain, and lack of control. I need to work.

I enter the small studio downstairs. My left heel is pounding while I stand with my legs apart, knees bent. All of my weight is in my pelvis. I am flattened against the wall as my left hand turns into a claw. I cannot find relief from the shape and energy of it. Finally, after much tension, vibrating, and heel pounding, I become quiet, facing east. I feel very old, sitting cross-legged, rocking. My hands are on top of my head. My hair feels dead, like straw.

I want to be bald, to make the top of my head bare. I push the hair away from the center on both sides. I am breathless, feeling completely suspended.

> **◖◗** *Light pours*
> *through the top*
> *of my head.*
> *Weightless*
> *I am inside*
> *and also outside*
> *my body.*

More and more frequently, I find my fingers making certain shapes while the visions come through me. They are very specific, each finger placed in exact relationship to the other fingers. Sometimes both hands move identically in this regard. Holding these hand positions is calming. Dusk arrives and I see.

[0] *A hole is carved*
a circle
in the top of my head
with a knife.
Two hands
pull out a rope
making a knot
pulling again.

Black women
dance. One begins
twirling.
She twirls down
into my body
now becoming
diffuse energy
traveling
up a center pole
toward the opening
in the top of my head.

A gigantic lion
born through
the hole
sits, his head
facing out
through the opening
into the universe
roaring toward infinity
his voice shaping
space.
His sound
his freedom
leave me breathless
teary.

Rabbit sits on his head.
Contemporary people
tumble
out of his mouth
down
into nowhere.

Again, a tug
a man
stiff in silver armor
appears
slit open.
My swan flutters out
of his entrails
nibbling the entire rim
of the opening
that invites
the emptiness
becoming the threshold
between this world
and that one.

I see purple
dark light
coming from the periphery
drawing a circle
around my third eye
swirling and evaporating
into unending nothing.

The hole
in the top of my head
its edges jagged
throbs, a gateway
for people floating
in and out
sometimes quickly.
Two babies

pass each other
in silence.

A spot midway down my spine burns. My third eye burns.

【()】 *Something wants to grow*
on the top of my head
a temple
a pagoda?

The moon skates
toward me
her shape exactly
filling the opening
at the top of my head.
Staying open
and drenched
in moon essence
the whiteness of liquid
sweeps down
into me
encircling, imbuing
becoming
the undulating ground.

Luminous light
washes over
from the edges
leaving in its wake
my third eye
pulsing
yellow on the outside
purple-blue
in the center.

It is 8:30 at night. I am in my room with Zachary's rabbit and Changa.

This rabbit, a special creature who is not easy to tame, has become a curious part of this process, of me in relationship to the visions. Tonight a thunderstorm shakes the trees. The house feels like the quiet once a woman begins labor. I feel it keenly. The visions now come and go more easily, appearing and disappearing with seemingly less cost.

[0] *I am*
an old Chinese man
tranquil
sitting cross-legged
my hands
resting on top
of my head.

Bending over
emerald green grass
spills from my crown
in ribbons
birthing spring
now summer
autumn
winter
landscapes unfolding
wide.

Now standing
scooting backward
bent over still
perfect pebbles
tumble
out of the top
of my head.
I see the sea
inside their shapes
lagoons.

October 10, 1982
The White House

My mind is clear. I continue to be conscious of everyone and everything even while I see visions. Before or after I see a vision, I know if Zach's shoes are untied or if David needs a haircut. I look carefully at each one of Theo's new paintings or at the designs for the next house. Today I see that Changa is limping and I must remember to call the vet. But my body feels so heavy, hard to move, and impossible to move quickly. I especially have trouble changing levels, as in getting up or sitting down. Today I sit in a timeless place, gazing at the marigolds Brian has brought me.

By evening the light from lamps is too bright. I feel as though light is coming out of my eyes as well. They ache terribly. There is too much light. I cannot use my eyes so I go to bed. I cannot sleep easily. Deep in the night I awaken, burning. I feel like hot coals, red hot.

> *I see*
> *directly in front*
> *of my face*
> *the left eye*
> *of a very old bird*
> *a glimpse*
> *of its beak*
> *staring at me*
> *powerfully, vividly.*
>
> *This eye*
> *stays open*
> *as dark men*
> *carry away pieces*
> *of my body, wrapped*
> *in white muslin.*

ARCHING BACKWARD

〔〕

November 4–7, 1982
Quonset Hut

I have come here to Rosalind's land to be totally alone. I do not want to speak or be spoken to. I do not want to see another person or to be seen by another. At sundown I sweep the hut, bring in the wood, and make the fire. The wind is blowing and I feel excited. Standing by the door, I sing out to the sky. As night falls, the wind becomes wild. I feel very spirited and sing out again, louder. Exhilaration meets with terror. I sense an immediate presence of a dark force sweeping down on my right and landing behind me. I turn, see nothing, and run inside. Holding the rabbit and singing grounds me fast.

At dusk I lie down in my sleeping bag. The rabbit is with me. I imagine the Old Woman sitting next to me. I imagine Theo outside, guarding the door.

(O) *Women kneel*
in a circle around
the fire.
Someone at my feet
pushes them
up and toward me.
They land flat
knees bent. Twice.
A river of blood
gently
flows from my yoni.
White feminine hands
push with effort
to part the dark masses
of flesh
on each side
of the riverbed
that carries my blood.

78

Down
deeper down
endlessly down
deep
so deep the blood runs
as the hands, in service
keep parting the weight.

The riverbed opens now
wide
the masses gone.
There is water. The woman
of the white hands
goes into the water.

The Old Woman
arches backward, dipping
her black hair in my blood.
She washes her hair
in my blood
as she arches
backward and over
my leg.

Covering her body
in my blood
the circle of women
get up one by one
holding hands
moving toward me
their hair falling
into the river
of blood.

They return to the fire
rubbing the blood
all over their bodies

shaking their heads
at the fire
as they dance.

Dancing and dancing
wilder, still wilder
the blood dries
molding
masks on their faces.
Their hair
caked in blood
sticks out
at the elephant man
who now dances
across the fire.

I am tired and my back has been burning for an hour. It is cold now and familiar here.

(O) *I see men*
pressing hard
pressing back the earth
with the sides of their hands.
They are pressing.
I am sinking.

The mounds make a circle
in the sandy soil.
There is black
firing up the center
a moving, spiraling
snake
circling and reaching
around and up
into nowhere.

The men's hands
keep pressing.
The Old Woman
arches
staggers backward
over my leg.
The river of blood
runs under her body
her mouth
open wide.
Urgently, she shifts.

A baby falls
out of the sky
into her mouth
and out of her yoni.
Now a small boy
he stumbles
to the pole
in the center
shimmying up into the sky.

The men's hands
support him
riding up
on the snake
as high up as the blood
river flows down
into infinity.

The night is quiet. I am not afraid. I awaken often to feed the fire and check the rabbit because it is so cold. Each time as I fall asleep, I feel intense aching all over my body, especially in my lower back. Putting my knees up helps the pain. The vibrations slow down. My heartbeat all the night through is very high, wide, and fast. Dawn approaches.

[O] *I see white*
the feminine hands
caressing
stroking in full
liquid movements
exquisite stones
emptying my mind
bringing bliss
briefly.

I feel strangely empowered. The rabbit repeatedly licks my left eye and my third eye. He does not lick my right one. I go back into my sleeping bag after tea and some cheese. My body quickly takes on the weight again. I feel heavier than I can describe, all over, enormous weight. I cannot move. I lie on my back, my hands resting on my stomach.

[O] *The rabbit digs*
between my legs
a hole in the earth.
Halfway in, he pulls
other rabbits
out of the earth
one by one.
The limp one
lies over my leg.

He pulls out huge warriors
males with beaks
bedecked in silver
shiny chest plates, hoods.

Up a ladder
out of the earth
they hurl their swords
into my yoni

curving and coming
out of my navel.
Sharp needles pierce
all of my openings.

I arch
throwing my head
backward
now forward
over on all fours.
Back and forth
the swords
become snakes
slithering into one.
Huge, long
it coils around me
leaving my hands
my arms
my legs and my feet
free
as it winds
around my neck
placing its head
in my mouth
and I leap
revealing my strength
in stunts
exact and strong.

Now I fall
forward, limp.
The warriors catch me
hitting my back.
Something starts spilling
out of my body.

Light.

The rabbit licks my eyes, staying a long time. As he leaves, I see.

[O] *Light is pouring*
out from my body.
Light is pouring
in rays, creating
a form on the earth
a form of a woman.

Somersaulting over
and into the form
I fill it, the edges
electric, emblazed.
Sitting up
I fill it
in long skirts
a headdress of gold.

The warriors are leaving.
I am sweeping
and shooing
the rabbits away.
Suddenly, I leave
the temple, weeping.
I am weeping.

I hear my own cries.

Rabbit licks my three eyes before and after visions. After an apple and some seeds, I feel dragged back to my sleeping bag. I feel so tired and weighted, so heavy.

[O] *Feminine hands*
the white ones
caress the stones

laying them
in a circle.
I come down
from the sky
onto the pole
in the middle.
I spin.

Roots grow
from my feet
branches reach
from my arms
from my mouth.
. My third eye
grows a branch
holding the rabbit
who sits on top
of a full green tree.

I go outside late afternoon, not really wanting to but feeling pulled. I follow the stone wall. I lean against a thin little tree that can barely hold me. Here in front of me is another tree, an old tree, its roots exposed, covered with moss, surrounded by rotting wood and a thick carpet of oak leaves. In the center I see a green egg, like the outer shell of a walnut. It is the eye of this forest circle. I sit in the circle facing the eye, with my arms and head reaching upward, weeping. Now looking down, I see.

[0] *I am naked*
lying face down
in the earth
my dark hair
mingling
with the dark of the earth
my tongue licking

the earth in great sweeps.

Undulating, I burrow
into the soil.
A tree grows
through me
cracking my pubis
piercing the base
of my spine
and out.

The four seasons
travel
through the tree.
I keep moving
my shoulders, my head
writhing.

Another tree grows up
into and through
my heart.
I am dead now
and suddenly quite still.
This tree grows tall
beyond the others.
At the top, in a nest
lays a very large egg.

I feel exhausted. I try to take the green egg—the one I found in the
forest circle—with me. I see it is full of black water and dirt, cracked at
the top. It will not budge. So I bring some of the rotting wood that
clings to it and some oak leaves back to my hut. I feel like making an
altar, though I never have made one before.

Just at sundown I create one near the fire pit. I put the cracked green
egg in the center, on top of the rotting wood. I put my porcelain swan

next to it, hang my diamond over it, light a candle, and, at the foot of it all, I burn the sage that Hannah left for me in a little handwoven pouch. I watch the exquisite coming of night, holding the rabbit. Singing many songs, I feel unusually peaceful. I sleep well for many hours. When I awaken, I see.

[O] *Faces of black people*
circle the tall tree
with me dead
in stillness
beneath.
They walk up the tree
quickly
locking their hands
their arms
making a basket
just below the nest.

Dark, limp, he slips
into their arms
carried down
to the earth
softly laid on top of me
dead Jesus
lifted down
from the cross.

Walking, robed in white
old men drag
a caisson with hay
with him, with me
into a very old city.

A great clump of earth
comes with us
under, around us

like the clump
I took
under the cracked green egg.

Suffering
he arches backward
over my leg.
I see the bones
of his neck
his collar bone
becoming
an altar piece
of delicate wood.

I awaken deep in the night, make a fire, eat an apple, hold the rabbit, and sing. I do a brief dance on white grass outside, under a halfmoon, hopping from enclosure to enclosure. These spaces are vividly marked by the shadows of the branches, such lovely shapes. I take a ride on the swing and unintentionally scare a little animal away.

I go back into my sleeping bag. The rabbit madly races around the hut and frequently insists on getting in the bag with me. Once, while licking my eyes, he bites the inside corner of my right eyelid. Later, while licking my hand, he bites the heel of my left thumb. Now he is forbidden to come near me the rest of the night.

I awake with the most dramatic vibrations inside. They are at the very front of my collarbone. I remember being here in this hut one and a half years ago, watching my collarbone burn. The vibrations are also going up my neck. My whole body is visibly shaking.

(●) *Suddenly*
the big egg
drops
into the earth

down
through the trunk
of the tree, with intent
burrowing
through tunnels
beige in color
a myriad of tunnels
that connect all places
a grand crisscrossing
a pattern complete.

At the center
of the earth
the egg starts spinning.
I read the languages
shining
on each facet
spinning, spinning
faster and faster
becoming a diamond.

The herdsmen descend
the old ladder
from the top
where they have been guarding
the nest with the egg
for thousands of years.

Their work is finished now.

Since I have come here, the quality, the deep texture of everything that exists in the universe feels the same. I do not wash. I sprinkle sage ash on my pillow. I wrap myself in a blanket covered with leaves and sticks. All food tastes the same. Light and dark, outside, inside, me, the night—we are all one. The world is of one matter and my flesh and blood are no different than the rabbit's or the leaf's.

This morning, with no more vibrations, shortness of breath, tiredness, back fire, I know a great resolution. I rise and want to wash, clean the hut, prepare to leave. My time here is complete. When the candle on the altar burns out, I will go.

MERGING

【】

November 14, 1982
The White House

> **[0]** *I see me*
> *lying on the earth*
> *spread-eagle*
> *made of diamond.*
>
> *I am a diamond.*
> *Light*
> *radiates*
> *from me.*

November 17, 1982
The White House

A colleague referred Judd to me as someone looking for employment who is great with children. He arrived for the interview on roller skates, wearing red suspenders. He seemed very interested in our situation. So now he lives on the third floor, writing his novel when he is not cooking, cleaning, or reading Tintin to the boys.

I come to my room at dusk to rest. I cannot sleep. I need something but I have no sense of what it might be.

> **[0]** *The Old Woman*
> *enters my room*
> *walking over there*
> *near the window.*
> *Now, passing the fire*
> *she sits*
> *on the edge of my bed.*

MERGING

After a long time
with great trepidation
I slowly place
infinitesimally place
my left hand
on her left hand
resting
on the bed.

Touching down
onto her hand
I feel heat
softness, immediately.

With her right hand
she rubs
hard
the back of my hand
rubbing, pushing the skin
toward me
revealing
the inside of me.

Filaments
strings of light
stretch open.

They are burning.

I lie still
deeply silent
a long time passing.
She brings
the flap of skin
back now
rubbing

*the top of my hand
burning.*

*Another long time
passes.
Slowly I take
my hand from hers
carefully, carefully
such a long journey
back.*

*Now I see my hand
black in shadow
coming toward me.
I receive it
with my right hand
gently pressing
finally embracing
kissing it.*

*My hand burning hot
the Old Woman gets up
walks away.
I see an empty space
where her back used to be.*

I go downstairs to dinner and am greeted by David at the bottom of the steps in his Yankee baseball cap and jacket. Lovingly and with much enthusiasm he gives me a present, an extraordinary dark crystal with an opening in the middle. He says he does not know why he chose this one at the craft fair, but he had to have it to give to me.

November 28, 1982
The White House

Judd is a tremendous help. He is consistent and loving with the
children, who seem to adore him, and he is definitely sensitive to my
experience of the energy. Yesterday, when I was walking with the staff,
the one Theo helped me make from a tree branch, and wondering how I
would ever make the trek back the few blocks to the house, I looked up
to see him, smiling, coming toward me with cheese and crackers to fuel
my system.

When I walk down our street I move slowly and sometimes need the
staff. The children and I have agreed on a way to speak about my
situation with others who might see me, those who are not close friends
or family. We say that I have back problems, which is not really lying.
They seem to understand that it would be uncomfortable for most
people to accept the explanation of intense energy inside my body
becoming fire and creating visions.

I am off-center all day. I know by afternoon that I will move in the
small studio downstairs. I know by evening that I will move "imagining"
the Old Woman witnessing me. I enter the studio, the bay windows on
my left, dark now, reflecting back my own image. I draw the curtains.
Standing in the middle of the room, I close my eyes.

> **[O]** *I see her*
> *sitting*
> *where I usually sit.*
> *I am too afraid.*
> *Her presence awesome*
> *I cannot turn*
> *my back*
> *toward her.*

I must touch
her left foot
with my left hand.
Everywhere I see her
she sits cross-legged
her left foot
looming large.

I must touch it.

I move back and forth across the room, from one end to the other, my feet shuffling in short, quick steps. My arms and hands follow this rhythm.

[ ] *I kneel*
before her
gigantic foot.
Almost not moving
I extend my hand
to touch it
terrified.

Now touching
the palm of my hand
the sole of her foot
she chops off my head
and right arm
at the shoulder.

Not moving
my left hand
I see fire
burning
from her foot
into my hand

96

shooting flames
burning
a long time passing.

I take back my hand.

I am very slowed down as I leave the room. My hand still feels hot as I write.

November 30, 1982
The White House

It is Friday morning and I do not teach. Adele meets with the students at her house on the mountain. I am relieved to be here alone. I hold the rabbit for a long quiet time in the kitchen.

■ *I see the Old Woman*
before me
with no back.
I put the rabbit
into that empty space.
Now tied to her
with a black ribbon
he jumps back
into my lap
as she walks away.

She dances
in the center
of my kitchen
scooting backward
arms reaching up
making small steps
in a square.

Wherever she goes
the ribbon connects her
to the rabbit
only if I hold him.

Now
I see her walking
up Village Hill Road
to the Quonset hut.

December 13–19, 1982
The White House

I have a teaching break now, until February. I need it badly as the energy is still so depleting. I don't know what I would do without Judd. Rosalind comes for a visit. We sit in the study. The world outside is white and ever so quiet. In here, we drink tea. Though it is impossible to describe these experiences, I try to tell her about my Old Woman and how much I honor her. Though she cuts, chops, and slices me to bits, which can be horrifying at one level, it is the energy itself that I know can destroy me, not the content of the visions. Somehow, within the context of the Old Woman's clear intention to see me through these trials by fire, even when she is actively involved with the burning, unraveling, and emptying, she repeatedly becomes my devoted guide. Her lack of sentiment when I am in the visionary state is welcomed.

Rosalind and I embrace at the door and I watch her walk out into the white snow, dressed in black as usual. At the end of the walkway, she turns, pauses, nods—almost smiling—and gets into her car. I come to my room.

◖◗ *The Old Woman*
tucks a pearl
into my third eye

way deep into the center
of the vortex
of the earth.

She cuts me
cuts my hands
cuts my legs
placing all the little pieces
in small leather pouches
left hand pieces
in one bag
right hand pieces
in another bag
leg pieces
in a dark yellow one.
Placing the pouches
in the hollow of her back
she saunters
away.

December 29, 1982
The White House

I get into the hot bathtub. I feel drawn to the water time after time as the energy builds and I inwardly prepare to see a vision. The heat, the weight, and the texture of it somehow support the part of me that surrenders to these experiences. The hot water becomes my medium.

◖◗ *The Old Woman*
kneels next to the tub.
Digging
deep into the vortex
of my third eye

she pulls out
the pearl
and swallows it.

I put my right hand
on the edge
of the tub.
She licks it
washing me clean.

Slowly placing
my hand on my face
I move it
clockwise
touching her coolness
onto my skin
my collarbone
my neck.

Now she bites
grinds
and swallows
my right hand.
I can see it
in her abdomen
in one piece
pushing
palm out
toward me.

Totally drained and in my slows, I can barely move. This is an absurd way to spend one's life. What am I doing? I can only proceed day by day with this energy. It is too much to sort out. I lie down in bed.

[0] *Now the Old Woman*
eats all of me

effortlessly
one quick swallow
a grey amorphous
mass.

I see me tumbling
down, endlessly
down, turning
until I land
in her center
my right hand
pushing, radiant
my left
just bones
scratching.

My physical health is so depleted, I long for the presence of someone who knows how to help me become strong again. I imagine most physicians would make a diagnosis related to psychological disturbance. Fear of the medical establishment's lack of understanding has kept me from seriously seeking help from them.

Finally, in response to Mother and Dad's concern for my health, Theo takes me to New York and I consult with two doctors at the department of neuropsychiatry at Columbia University Medical School. It is confirming to hear the director of the program tell me that he believes the source of my physical problems is kundalini energy. Three people have mentioned this word to me since these experiences began. The doctor briefly explains the meaning of the word. He says it is a Hindu term used to describe an initiation process by which an individual awakens into the fullness of nonordinary perception through the experience of an infusion of energy burning through the entire body. He has little else to say other than suggesting that I read Dante's *Inferno*. Apologizing for his lack of time, he writes something in a folder and quite genuinely wishes me luck.

Though I am very relieved to think that what is happening to me has a
name, is a concept with a history, I do not have enough energy to study.
And reading is very difficult. I am also aware of not wanting to interfere
with what I now trust is a deeply organic process. These visions are not
chaotic. They seem to have an order. Because of my vivid imagination, if
I were to read about similar experiences in other people's lives I might
unconsciously absorb their descriptions, and then I could no longer
know that my experiences are authentic.

I recognize my austerity here, but I trust it. I sense a great need for
strengthening a particular boundary as I am taken more fully into a time
and space with no boundary.

SEARCHING

【】

December 31, 1982–January 6, 1983
The White House

The house is empty. The holidays are over. Theo has flown to the Bahamas to paint. I would love to go with him but I cannot. Making the choice to stay here highlights a split I often feel since this initiation began. I am torn between the visionary in me and the lover or mother or teacher in me. Increasingly I need to be alone when I embody a vision retreat. And this is the only time I have while Zach and David are on vacation with Nathan.

I prefer going away somewhere for this round, but I cannot locate a retreat center or situation in which I would feel safe and simultaneously have my needs met. Besides, that kind of research is too tiring. And the Quonset hut is too cold. So I stay at home and unplug the phone. Now the house looms big, cold, and dark downstairs. I bring everything I will need up here as I prepare my own room for a seven-day silent retreat. While I am looking for my old grey woolen tights, I find Grandmere's rose silk shawl on the top shelf of my closet. I like it suddenly and feel that I need it. Draping it over me I lie down, closing my eyes.

[0] *In the bath*
weeping
I swing
way above
another tub
where Theo
sits.

He is gesturing
toward me
in space.
As I touch
my legs
they evaporate.

The slows come quickly.

[0] *I place a circle*
of protection
around the house
a black circle
on the ground.
Giant dolphin scales
instantly grow
translucent, strong
especially vivid
in the upper, front left
corner of my room
the southwest.

I see my people
in their places
guarding me
the Old Woman
at the foot of the bed
on the green pillow
to the right.

I greet Hannah
at the door.
She bows. I bow.
I walk her
in a slow spiral
into the very center
of the room
in front of the fireplace.

I see Theo, Rosalind
Rosa, Mother
and Adele

standing in a circle
at the end of long
silver poles
radiating
from the center
where Hannah stands
creating
a unified system
with tension
and delicacy.
This inner circle
sings of life
the outer circle
behind
of death
Nanette, Grandmother
Uncle Ray Stone.

Hannah shifts
to the empty place
by the fire.
I step
into the center
with the Old Woman.

We are wrapped
together
in the frayed, rose
silk shawl.

I see light
raining, raining
out of the base
of the sternum
from the one on top

SEARCHING

I do not know
if it is she or me
into the other's body
a lovely
resplendent spray.

[0] *My hands*
suddenly shoot up
the left one
higher.

Now light pulses
from both palms.
I am weeping.
My left hand
gives way
landing
between my legs.

With a black
bottlebrush
it scrubs
the inside
of my uterus
spilling out
the sexual.
The entire cavity
absorbing blackness
deflates
shrunken and shriveled.

I am exhausted and aching all over. It is hard to write all of this, to remember it, but since the first vision two years ago, each time I feel compelled to write. I light the fire, eat an apple and some cheese, and feel too tired. I am so glad I brought food up here. Again I lie down.

[()] *A formidable person*
both male and female
in a long sweeping and dark
wine-red robe
winds string
around my wizened
black female organs
and holds them
by the yoni stem
up high.

Spinning them
back and forth
between his hands
the hermaphrodite
laughing, teasing
offers them
reaching wide
toward each man
in a circle.

Grinning
he takes them back
barely turns
and offers them
to the next one.
Now they are laid
in the center
oozing black liquid
black blood.

The men run

over them.
Shuddering, I see
one digging his heels
into my flesh.

They circle in
close
each with a big stick
held across
the back of his thighs.

Dancing in a circle
faster, faster
heat rising
they climb
toward orgasm
without release.
They lie face down
piling their hands
onto my uterus
in the center.

More woman now
the hermaphrodite
takes it away
and sits down
on a stool
before the fire
passing it
under her seat
three times
from back to front.

Rising, she dances
elegantly
wearing my female organs

on top of her head
a headdress.

Now I am celibate.

I am waiting, wrapped in the rose silk shawl.

[O] *I see white light*
spraying
from David's dark crystal
down into the emptiness
where my uterus
once lived.

I am restless, hot, and not at peace. My body can barely move. I wish I did not have to eat. Food hurts my stomach and mostly I am not hungry. I sleep and awaken with a feeling of peace, deep peace. Emptiness. A vow of celibacy feels correct.

[O] *Now I see me*
jump
up from behind
the Old Woman
my torso
fitting perfectly
in the hollow of her back
legs hanging
under her skirt
arms hugging
her waist.

Today as I literally stand in the center of my room, I again see the silver-pole circle. I move very slowly, counterclockwise. I feel ancient. I sing a low, quiet song. There is a slight pull of my head and arms upward. I am too exhausted. I lie down and feel myself falling asleep. I lie in a specific position on my stomach, my right arm at my side, my left hand under my head. I cannot move and do not want to. This is correct. I experience continuous and powerful quickening for hours.

At dusk I light the fire, make an altar, and put my diamond on it. I begin slowly turning in front of the fire, taking off my clothes. I scrape off, fling out, throw down, shaking my hands until they are numb, all the time turning, turning. I am fierce, hissing and flashing my palms at arm's length, protecting this space. Aggressive, loud sounds fill the room. My footwork precise, I spin faster and faster, creating a great circle around me, a circle of giant white dolphin scales, clearest in the southwest corner. It is clear, all clear, between the edge and me.

Feeling dizzy, I stop the dance. Sitting close to the fire, I am strong, lithe, dark. I am a woman warrior. I wrap the rose silk shawl around me. I realize that I am the result of the merging of the Old Woman and me. I feel a rush of sadness, wondering if that means she is gone, no longer my guide.

( ) *I see*
a young Native American woman
wearing green
sitting on the edge
of my bed.

Curious
she takes my hand
turning it
round and round
like a screw
inspecting
all sides.

She scrapes back
toward my heart
strips of skin
below my wrist
like petals
of a flower.
My hand
goes into her mouth
now all of me, down
inside her.

But below
inside her, I land
in the belly, now dark
dark red
of the Old Woman.
Turning
my hand pushes out.

Suddenly
my radiant hand
pushes right through
the wall
of her old tired stomach.
Emerging, I stand
tall
lean and healthy.

Standing up, naked, pulling the silk shawl around me, I walk to the southwest corner of the room. I am flooded with images and thoughts of the Southwest. Quaking, I get into the hot water, knowing I must go to Santa Fe. Though I know no one there, I just know that I must go. Simultaneously I feel reassured, remembering that I have not acted on any other visions previous to this time. Just this once, I must.

[O] *The Old Woman kneels*
by the tub
far away, near my feet.
Now she is faceless
a night void.

I see the edge of her hood
in silver
dripping into the water
dissolving
now all of her
dissolving
into my body
entering me.

I open my mouth
wide. Emerging
and turning toward me
she paints
with a fine brush
starting at the top
of my third eye
going around
down
to the right
small, yellow
petals
down
to the midpoint.

Now going up to the left
she paints more
petals, blue petals.
It is the sun
no, a flower.

I am her witness.

She forms each mark
in front of me
as though the painting
appears
on her third eye, yet
it is clearly on mine.
I can feel it.

Now white light
shining
out of my third eye
must touch her third eye.
Maybe it does.
Putting my hands
on the sides of my face
I feel her hands
under mine
a good-bye.

Floating above
my light touches
down
on a city
in the Southwest.

I am too tired. The weight is unbearable as I walk again out into the night hall, into the bathroom, into the hot water. I light the candle as always before getting in. Small rituals such as this one have become mandatory somehow, a call for impeccability in the simple gestures that precede and follow the receiving of the visions.

SEARCHING

[O] Now in the water
I find
the Old Woman
with me
facing me.
Opening my mouth
wide
she places
the dark crystal
on my tongue.

She commands:
Put your whole head
under the water.
I refuse.
She insists:
Put your whole head
under the water.

Resisting, I take the pins out, my hair falling. I am deeply afraid. I know I must, telling myself this is just a bathtub, but I feel increasingly terrified. I cry. I beg for help.

[O] I threaten
it will take forever
realizing
the Old Woman
will wait
forever.

The fear, the terror, is indescribable. Finally I find myself stretching my hands to the front end of the tub, kneeling over, knowing that this is the position. After much wailing, I do it. I put my entire head under and up three times. The last time, I rise all the way up onto my knees, water pouring from my hair, my face up. I pull the hair away from my third eye and hear myself singing, "Hi-yi-yi-yi," with spirit and celebration.

> [O] *Vividly I see*
> *high up*
> *through my third eye*
> *a man*
> *with a short black beard*
> *standing, holding*
> *on his right hip*
> *a little dark girl*
> *wrapped*
> *in a red shawl.*
> *He stares at me*
> *penetrating.*

This vision is crystal clear. I see it for a long time, all the while chanting, "Hi-yi-yi-yi!" I now know to go and receive the child. He will give her to me. This message seems obvious. My thoughts register in a thick Russian or German accent.

I prepare to leave this house. Finding my old heavy black cape and packing a bag of oranges and seeds, I go. No one must know. Because of the children, someone must know. I go to Rosalind, leaving her my journals of visions and cryptic instructions in case my boys need me. Now I wait at the airport. Now I am on the plane. The woman to my right asks me if I am a nun. I answer yes. We talk together.

After the first and most potent look at the man and child, the image is almost constant. Once an old woman was lurking behind them. Maybe it is she I am going to meet. It might be at a bus or a train station in Santa Fe. If the Albuquerque airport is very modern, I don't think that is it. I see a very specific place because of the details of the vision. Another woman near me on the plane is reading a book entitled *Vision*. She lives in Santa Fe. The rational part of me does not believe I am doing this. My clear self knows that I am choosing to do this and it is right. May I be able to see what I am ready to see.

I sit in a corner of the Albuquerque airport and watch as if I am witnessing in the movement studio. A woman who looks exactly like Rosalind, in black, her white hair pulled into a bun, sits nearby. We never make eye contact. I feel protected by her presence. The texture of the furniture and counters is not like the vision. I sense the man and child are not here. As I leave, so does the woman in black.

It is cold here with snow and too much concrete. I find a hotel room in Santa Fe. I awaken at dawn with terrific pressure behind my eyes. Now I experience a heated conflict between my personality and my clear self. I place my ego self on a chair that is across the room on my right. My clear self is placed opposite on the left. It is a battle about inflation and deflation, about the threat of self-betrayal, about trust. Severely challenged, my clear self emerges intact, in charge. Now I must see.

[0] *The Old Woman*
leaning against my left knee
lets tobacco fall
from paper
paper
to roll a cigarette.
I see above her
a strange wheel
shiny, but wooden
with a handle
that turns clockwise
a gambling wheel.
A tobacco shop?

I see
a small Oriental woman
lifting
three very thin
silver poles
like antennae
up, between her hands.
Now she rolls
thin pastry
on a counter
filling
rolling again
cutting it
into pieces.
A bakery?

I see
a blinding yellow light
emerging from the left
black
ski-shapes
tall and rising.
A doorway?

I see
terrific confusion
small, old planes
landing, taking off
painted
green and brown
in camouflage designs.
Soft energy moves
until I can no longer see.
An airfield?

I see
a big rabbit or person
wearing many clothes
on crutches
coming out of a door
followed by two others
in wheelchairs.
I squeeze past them
through a door.
A hospital?

The pressure is still great, but it is too hard now to see. I will go out and begin my search. I learn that there is no train station. I go to the bus station. This feels right. The vintage of the furniture, the style and texture, closely resembles the vision. When I first sit down, the sun is coming up, glaring in through the door. Two men, the silhouettes of their skis looming just behind them, come into the room—the first clue, found. People become familiar as they wait, come, and go. There is one old Native American man, cross-eyed, with whom I feel a connection. Many old men are rolling their own cigarettes. I see several game machines in the room. One, which is a wheel, is on the wall. Another clue grounded. I feel completely comfortable here.

Later in the day, I am hungry but am afraid to leave. What if the man arrives with the child and I am gone? I speak to the man at the counter, explain that I am waiting and carefully describe the travelers:

[ ] *a man*
with a short black beard
standing, holding
on his right hip
a little dark girl
wrapped in a red shawl.

My bases covered, I go across the street and into an old interesting building with small shops. I say to a man with a short dark beard, who stands near the door, that I am hungry. Where might I eat? He gestures to his left. I follow his gaze and see a Korean woman arranging her booth, adjusting a thin awning that is held up by slim, metal poles. Now she begins to make egg rolls, rolling the dough, filling it, cutting it. I am on. I step into her space and sit in a big wooden booth. Looking up I see a large wooden rabbit, painted white, on a shelf above me. I feel protected. When the light shifts toward night, I find a room in a nearby hotel, spacious and old.

Another day, and to make sure the bus station is the right place, I spend the first half of it waiting in a wing of the hospital where orphans are occasionally brought. But it is too modern and does not look like the physical space in which I might see:

> **[()]** *a man*
> *with a short black beard*
> *standing, holding*
> *on his right hip*
> *a little dark girl*
> *wrapped in a red shawl.*

I return to the bus station and after reminding the man behind the counter to tell the travelers to wait if they should come in my absence, I go to the Korean woman for lunch. While eating hot vegetable soup and dark bread under the protective gaze of the rabbit, I realize that I have been staring through an opening out into the area with shops, at a sign that says Contemporary Vision. I am drawn to see what is there, the name feeling familiar. As I walk into the space, I am surrounded by paintings of some of my visions. I am stunned and profoundly moved.

I speak with Jack, the gallery owner from South Florida, patron of the Mexican artist whose work pulses around me. I meet his wife, Estelle, a tall, exceptionally beautiful woman. They are interested in my journey. I am interested in theirs.

On my way back to the bus station, I pass the old Native American man, the one with whom I feel a connection, the one who is cross-eyed, whom I have seen several times in the bus station. He is speaking to someone. I find myself stopping, waiting, standing next to him. Now we speak. I tell him I am looking for a man with a child. He asks how I know to come to Santa Fe. I touch my third eye lightly and say, through visions. He suggests we sit down together, have coffee, and talk.

His name is Ben. He tells me of his life and the life of his people and of his knowing that his race is dying and that there is no longer hope. He tells me that years ago, in great conflict, he took a little girl about the age of three, whose mother had died, to a hospital in Santa Fe. He left her there to be cared for in an orphanage. When she was grown, she returned to the pueblo. He invites me to come to his pueblo, where he is one of the chiefs, for All King's Day. Returning to the bus station, I spend the rest of the day waiting. Jack stops by to check on me as evening comes.

Another day and Estelle drives me to the pueblo. We are warmly welcomed into the home of my new friend. As he lights a fire in the corner of his room, I feel so deeply stirred that I cannot really listen as he shows us, tells us, shares with us in this intimate space where he lives alone.

We go to the feast. I see immediately, among the Native American women preparing and serving an abundant meal, one woman. She looks different, with strong Oriental features, a refined beauty. She works alongside the others, preoccupied, moving differently. She is unlike the others. The chief sees me, my gaze riveted. He slowly leans toward me, not looking at me, and says, "She is the child, grown up."

The next day, he walks me to the bus that will take me to the airport. As I say goodbye, he hands me a picture of himself as a young man.

[◖] *He is the man*
with a short black beard
standing, holding
on his right hip
a little dark girl
wrapped in a red shawl.

As I wait in the Albuquerque airport to board, I see an older woman in a wheelchair. She is pushed right in front of me. Immediately I see a person squeezing through a door on crutches, followed by a man in a wheelchair with a cast on his leg—another clue to help close this search. On the plane, as we ascend, I look down and see on the ground, and then a few in the air, little army planes in camouflage colors and designs.

Perhaps I am thirty years late, or maybe the little girl is me. I am so glad, so very glad I have made this journey. I do not yet understand all that has happened. Throughout, I have felt totally protected and deeply directed.

ECSTASY

【】

January 21, 1983
The White House

[O] Looking into
a wood stove
warmed
by the coals
seething
after a blaze
I see
a gigantic snake
deep red, marked
licking himself
round and beautiful.

How can he live
in fire?
I remember
I know
closing the door
noticing
a part of his body
sticking out.

January 26, 1983
The White House

[O] I have an enormous
and long lingam
erect.
I have also
my yoni.

I am whole.

124

January 30–31, 1983
The White House

Hannah comes. She brings the boys a poster of a rock star. They are very excited. David says: "Look, he is seeing visions!" Zachary clasps his hands in front of his chest and says: "Maybe when I grow up I will see visions, too." Hannah helps them hang it on David's wall.

Lawrence comes in to get the children ready for a sledding adventure on the big hill behind the college. We cannot find David's hat. Finally they waddle out the door, completely covered except for their eyes, one chocolate pair and one blue like today's sky. Hannah makes some soup as she tells me about her trip to Nicaragua, the orphanage there where she worked, and the great fear among the families. When I hear about people's suffering, I am aware that my sensitivity to other's pain is becoming magnified beyond description. This energy teaches me in such subtle but clear ways that we are all the same. I know this.

I realize I must take advantage of the boys being out for the afternoon and let the energy through. The pressure is strong. Regardless of content, I am always relieved when the energy is released. Hannah watches the fire. I step into the bathtub, feeling weak and aching terribly.

[O] *I see way below*
and a bit in front
a person flinging
live, white doves
at my third eye.
The doves slap me
there and fall away.

I receive the blows.

Now I hold one
pecking, opening
my third eye
wide.

When the boys return, Hannah serves soup for all of us, then reads to them at bedtime. The apartment feels cozy tonight. Maybe I will be able to sleep deeply now.

After teaching a small group in the studio at home this morning, I take a walk in the woods, ending at dusk at Paradise Pond. Only one person is skating, backward. I go up the many steps and into the Crew House studio. This room is abundant in its emptiness. When I first moved to the area, Rosalind welcomed me and offered me time in this space. It was perfect for my Authentic Movement therapy groups then, for my more private work with Rosa later, and now we meet here weekly for the large group training work at the Institute. Sometimes I bring the boys here, late in the afternoon, after the college dance classes are over, and we run round and round. Today I cannot run. I lie down.

> **[○]** *I see me*
> *here*
> *in my corner*
> *witnessing students.*
> *Up high*
> *I see down*
> *wide.*
>
> *Moving*
> *out and away*
> *I turn*
> *seeing in my place*
> *a creature.*
> *It is the Old Woman*
> *with a huge beak*
> *jutting*
> *out the top of her head.*
> *With hollow back*
> *she is wrapped*
> *in my rose shawl.*

She comes to me
biting my head
into small pieces
creating a smooth arc
with her beak
where my neck
used to be.

Now I see me
back in my corner
in the lap of the Old Woman.
Cradling me
her body a boat
her skirts
lapping
lapping around me
caressing until
I am whole again.

In her lap
arching backward
I dive into her chest
coming out
through her yoni
facing forward
locked
in the vice
of her bones
my head
of bird and fish
my mouth open
wide.

I see me
stuck and weeping.
With compassion
I hesitate and reach

stretching, pulling
gathering
receiving me.

A birth.

February 6, 1983
The White House

Not knowing, not knowing enough about this process, I am constantly
wondering if I can endure the not knowing. I can only know what my
direct experiences teach me. In the meantime, the rounds of visions
keep coming. Often just as I begin to recover from one round, the signs
of the next round appear—pressure behind my eyes, fire in my back,
and my movement slowing down. There is no time for rest, recovery,
and integration. The experiences themselves deplete me, no matter how
ecstatic. I am so glad Judd is with us. He helps constantly.

Will the visions ever be about other people's suffering, about the pain in
the world, not always about my disintegration? How much longer will I
be able to work? Are the children having a normal enough childhood?
Will my body ever be healthy again? Should Theo and I seriously try to
make a life together in a traditional way? How can I marry and con-
ceive his child when I do not know if I will live through this?

After a day and a half of weeping, I step into the hot water, feeling
terrified.

I ask for the Old Woman.
Hannah enters the room
letting the rabbit in.
No. I want
the Old Woman.
Words tell me:

She is you.
Looking down
I see her
at the base of my spine
sitting
legs crossed.

I inhale.
She breathes
into my center black pole.

Now I exhale
three times
a sound erupting
from the base of my spine
up and out
through the top
of my head.

A siren
I can make this
sound forever.

February 7-9, 1983
The White House

[O] *I lie down*
my legs open.
A javelin, silver-white
flashing, long
comes hurling
into my yoni
thrusting
out the top of my head

tipped
with red fire
over and over.

Theo comes to me
embracing me.
Standing
he becomes an old man
in an instant
falling dead.

Three rabbits crawl
into his mouth, pulling
out his tongue.
One rabbit moves
back and forth
dragging tongues
from Theo to me
one by one
into my yoni
up to the tip of my sternum.
Laying them there
crossing them
his teeth cut holes
stitching them in place.

There are three.

Now a man
of gold and muscle
pushes my thighs
open
presses them down
enters me
the tip of his lingam
on fire.

Reaching the tip

of my sternum
his lingam ignites
the tongues.
The tongues
burn back and into
the spot on my spine
where long ago
the circle of blood
breathed
where yesterday, today
my body
burns
and burns.

This man of gold and muscle
loves me
sucking my nipples
on fire
sucking out a person
swallowing her.

His lingam
burns
across the place
where my legs
and torso meet
flaming
now entering
my mouth
igniting
my vocal chords.

Instantly I know
tremendous pressure
behind my third eye
creating
a royal blue velvet

mandala
bordered in golden pins.

A rabbit
glistening, coated
in tiny crystals
emerges.
Now I am
all of me
just crystals
nerves ending
in light.

A cut is made
down my neck
to the top of my sternum.
Opened
I see the tip
of the lingam
no longer ablaze.

I see the Old Woman
at the base of the lingam
tiny, arching backward
over its length
rocked
by the rhythm
of its movement
in and out.
My breastbone
opens, opens
wide
into a charred space
empty.

The channel is clear.

I see me magnified
hair long and wet
squeezed out
of an opening
barely fitting.

Giant size
I lie out flat.
I am the mountains
the valleys.
People build campfires
on my nipples
my navel.

The first lingam
attached at my yoni
presses into
the center shaft of me
straight up
with the head of a duck
pushing out through
the top of my head
the beak spinning
spinning
turning into a flower
opening.

It is dusk again. I must get into the hot water, now.

[O] *Within a great white*
circular light
I see the soles
of white feet
facing me

a white body
curled up on its back
behind the feet.

The feet open
just a little
revealing a yoni
open, just a little.
I feel fear
great fear.

A cat shoots
red flames from its paws
toward the left
of this fully white figure.
A bulb
above to the right
emits
an electrical charge.

A great and giant head
pushes up and out of the water.
Now I see
the whole man
erect, virile
potent.

I know him.

Energy pulses
out through my third eye
on every exhale.
I see an explosion
deep blue
creating an entire universe
deep blue
stars everywhere
becoming soft

vapors, pale rose
fading into light.

I see the Old Woman
so small
pale blue
slung over the great lingam
wet and limp
her journey exhausting.
I inhale
and she inflates
deflating
as I exhale.

We are one
the same.

I begin to sink. My hands, now my feet, now arms and legs slowly
become paralyzed. I cannot move.

[0] *The blue spirit*
arching backward
hangs over
the great lingam.

The candle goes out. The total darkness is soothing. I am not moving at
all. I wonder how I will get back to my room. For a very long time I
move out of the water and back into my bed. I am sinking.

[0] *I see the white feet*
opening
the yoni
opening
the lingam
erect, all

on a vital white being
both male and female
hermaphroditic
the looping of energy
into and through
the organs
the openings
the complete ouroboros.

This being climbs out
onto the edge of the sun
standing
toes curled on its rim
arching backward
diving
into the brilliance
of white light.

Ecstasy.

My mind is clear but my body is limp, unbelievably limp. I cannot open my eyes, direct my hands, or sit up. Judd brings crackers and tea but I cannot chew or drink. As I lie down to sleep, I am flooded with visions, loose and flowing. There is a last whirl of light, bright and blazing, coming from everywhere. I see it. I hear it. One light is central and blinding, completely white. I am it.

BIRTHING

【】

March 2, 1983
High Meadow

I feel that I am dying. The boys are with Nathan for two weeks. I am desperate for help. I sense that people who believe they can help or wish to try can easily misunderstand this energy, mostly because it has not been directly experienced by them. They can, without intention, interfere energetically, emotionally judge, or intellectually interpret what is happening.

My resistance to seek help in the last year and a half melts under the pressure of my terror. I make an appointment with Alex, a man Angela heard about who has had direct experience of this energy over a period of twenty years. She takes me to see him in his office, a modest and unpretentious space. He is kind and reassuring. He insists that I see no more visions for a while and that I completely focus on recovering from such violent attacks of the energy. He tells me to walk until I collapse from physical exhaustion, to try not to nap so that I will be truly tired at night, to be outside as much as possible, and to eat meat. Finally I can call on someone who seems to know about this. I feel a certain relief.

March 3, 1983
High Meadow

Alex is right. Even lying or sitting still can be an instant invitation toward the visionary state. When the danger seems too great, when I cannot by my own will stay in this reality, Theo takes me with him. He puts me in front of him while he is building the cabinets for the new house. I see his hands, meticulously, artfully crafting the fine edges, working the wood as if it were clay. He talks to me, constantly trying to engage me so I will not be pulled away by the energy. I know this, understand what he is doing and yet need him to do it because I cannot always stay present through my own will.

Today it is unbearably difficult. I cannot keep my eyes open. Theo is working at his drafting table. I try walking in the woods nearby. I stagger. I cry. When I stop, the silence is stunning. As I walk I realize I am holding the delicacy of a new form and its breathless fragility. Simultaneously I carry the stiffness, the death of the old form.

March 4, 1983
High Meadow

Theo and I groom the horses before he goes to work on the house plans. I brush Dream, stroking her coat with my left hand as I feel and hear the brush moving across her belly under my right hand. Being so dependent on Theo worries me. I tell him I will try walking to Angela's house a mile away. Walking haphazardly, I stop and hear dead birch leaves rustling on a branch. I walk again and stop. I hear a bird sing. The smell of the fresh air is stirring. I walk again. I hear a train. I see a tiny waterfall. I cannot get all the way to her house. I am too tired and sit by the side of the road next to the waterfall. Waiting for me, because Theo phoned to tell her I was coming, Angela comes by in the car and picks me up. I really cannot bear to be seen this way, even by her.

March 7, 1983
High Meadow

When I work with my hands, I do best. I draw the tree roots, knit with smooth big wooden needles, and work in clay. I learn I must stay in the present as if it is a command. Any thinking that ventures off into past or future is disastrous—I immediately feel pulled out of my body and into the direct experience of seeing visions. I feel tenuous, depleted beyond description, and often hopeless. I need time. I know I do. I must make it. I have two sons.

Hannah comes to drive me to Alex's office. The blizzard creates a whiteness everywhere that reflects my inner space. She talks to me constantly, quietly, trying to keep me with her. Her humor about this task is perfect.

Waiting for Alex, I notice the new skylight above the table where I sit, the edges still unfinished. It is very difficult to hold my head up and keep my eyes open here. I do not know him well and I feel embarrassed. He asks me questions about the Institute, the children, Theo and his friends, and I ask him about this energy. I feel relieved to hear him talk about it, its presence in all cultures, and its gift. I know its gift. May I survive to integrate it.

Back at High Meadow, I collapse on the couch. Hannah makes tea. I cannot resist. I see.

> **()** *Four transparent figures*
> *beckon to me.*
> *I move the essence of me*
> *into one of them.*
> *Still alive*
> *I do not have to die*
> *to become*
> *another form.*
>
> *This is good.*

March 19, 1983
High Meadow

Again I have to close the Institute early. It is devastating to me but I have no choice. I cannot forgive myself for imagining I could do it and then for not doing it, not completing the work with my students again! Adele is guiding them in this time of transition. And the children—

David will stay with Judd at home for two more weeks, then he will stop school and come be with us here. He is not happy about leaving school but there is no other alternative. He does love it here on the farm and he has been promised frequent visits with his friends here and at home. Theo will help him finish the year's school work. Zachary will come here now. He is too young and missing school is no problem. He is learning to read, so I will read to him. I can do that. And we will snuggle. We both love snuggling.

March 26, 1983
High Meadow

Theo's patience and devotion are astounding. I cannot imagine what I would do without him. Zachary and I have a morning schedule after Theo goes to work. We read on the couch by the fire for a long time. We have a snack at the big round smooth wooden table that Theo built. We walk in the woods. Today Zach plays with slabs of ice melting at the edge of the pond. I watch the irregular forms become formless, liquid, cold and moving. He likes to taste the pieces of ice with his tongue. We miss David so much. We talk to him every evening on the phone and play with him here every weekend. He tells us about catching the ball on first base three times in yesterday's game. He reads us a poem he wrote in school.

May 22, 1983
High Meadow

I am better. Something has shifted, or sifted inward. I spend as much of the day as I can playing with the boys outside. They are my anchors. I experience my weight differently. I walk and move in wonder at the subtle newness of each gesture, each sensation. Though my voice is still very thin, with no strength or volume, this body, my body, becomes new. The crocuses are up.

Theo wants us to stay here with him on the farm for the summer. I want to. I believe it is the best place for me and the children at this time. I have been completing business at the Institute by mail, which has mostly meant correspondence with each student in an effort to correctly bring closure to my relationship with each of them. Now I begin by phone arranging to sell our home. I cannot manage it alone anymore. Judd will help us. He will do all of the packing. I must trust him to do it the way I ask, attending to what can be thrown out and what must be stored. He will visit us here in the summer. When we move back in late August in preparation for the boys' return to school, I will find an apartment.

September 19, 1983
The River House

The summer was renewing. I became stronger—strong enough to not see visions and to stay in the realm of daily reality most of the time. Alex and I had several important meetings in which I learned more about my own ability to ground the energy. I continue to tire very easily and am unable to be out in the world for any length of time. Zachary and David are back in school. Theo stayed in the Berkshires to work. We each miss him very much.

We have moved to a village outside of town, into the upstairs apartment of a lovely old renovated house. Because I can't work, it is going to be tight financially, but I am so relieved to have no other responsibility except mothering, which continues to be the most grounding, the most important. I get the children off to school in the mornings, lie on the couch most of the day in my beige "vision-robe," as Zachary calls it, and get upright and dressed in order to be here for them or with them until their bedtime. Many boys live and play on this charming old street. Rosalind lives at the top of the hill. I can hear the river running past the window in my room here upstairs.

We have invited no new students to the Institute this fall. The women from the first two years are continuing on their own, meeting regularly. I am so grateful to Adele, who keeps holding it all together as well as directly supervising the individual work. But I can no longer work. The cumulative effect of this energy on my body has become significant. I just cannot try again. There is a great chasm between the gifts of this process in terms of my perceptual experiences and its effects upon my now diminished body.

Today I walk up the hill with my staff to see Rosalind. This takes a very long time. I notice the sound of my footsteps for the first time. She sits me on the earth with two boxes of pansies and suggests I plant them. The purples and pinks in the petals seem unusually bright and vivid. I see her working nearby in the garden, hear Bach playing on the stereo inside, and begin to dig in the earth. I like this.

Indoors now, I can hear the screen door slam as Rosalind goes in and out, talking to the dog. As I lie down, I experience myself as separate from my heartbeat.

> **[0]** *My mind*
> *unrolls, revealing*
> *nothing.*
> *Unfolding*
> *into emptiness*
> *the spiral*
> *spins, becoming*
> *fragments*
> *of star light*
> *celestial and fine.*

September 28, 1983
The River House

I am trying still another diet because of continuous stomach pain. It takes much time and effort to learn what I can eat, how to prepare it, and how to simultaneously cook for the boys. I can see the river from the window in the kitchen of this apartment while I cook. This helps me. Nancy comes for dinner, bringing banana bread, David's favorite.

There is no moon tonight, no white sphere in the sky. I am aware of a gradual craving for white, for clear space, for as little density as possible. I love my room here upstairs—white walls, white ceiling and floor, white comforter and sheets. There is nothing in here but the bed and the night table and the coiled white empty vase on the floor by the door. I lie down and close my eyes.

[●] *I am lost, not clear*
edges muted.
I pull a handful
of hair, gently
in slow motion
no effort, no pain
from above my right ear.

Looking in the mirror
I see
a large open hole
with a membrane
covering
only some of it
an antechamber below
behind
with dark blood
old blood
along the bottom edge.

Inside I see
empty space.

My mind is empty.

Peace, complete peace, fills me. I feel empty and clear, reborn.

November 20, 1983
The River House

I have more strength in terms of dealing with the outside world. I had two good conferences with the children's teachers. I care about each of these women and they so visibly care about our boys. I love their little school and the connection I have always had with the people there. Both David and Zachary are doing fine.

I have been experiencing strong "attacks" of energy in my heart. When they come, I feel overwhelmed, literally, by the physical sensation in that area of my body. I feel such expansion of love that I fear I cannot hold it. It is intense, indescribably uplifting. It is helpful to talk with Alex about this. Now in the bathtub, I find my hands, palms together, fingers pointing up, in front of my heart.

[O] *I see my heart*
red, in flame.
In the center
barely visible
a man sits
the Buddha
surrounded by my fingers
petals opening
burning white.

December 5, 1983
Miami Airport

I have been visiting my parents because Dad is so ill. I was very worried about making such a trip, but I did it. Theo took me to the airport and will stay with David and Zachary. Hannah will pick me up. Though physically weak, the new energy enabled me to be present in this crisis in an expanded and integrated way. Gratitude. I feel so much gratitude.

I am alone in this airport, waiting to board my flight home. I look up and see the little girl I tried to find in Santa Fe staring at me. She is now seven or eight years old. There next to her is her father, *exactly* as I saw him in the vision. And there is the old grandmother, very familiar—the three of them. The child and I simply stare at each other. The grandmother combs her hair. I am stunned.

It is time to board. The child sits in the seat directly in front of me, the father next to her and the grandmother on the aisle. They speak Spanish. As I get up to walk in the aisle I see the father, with such gentleness, pull the long black hair from the sleeping girl's face. The grandmother watches lovingly. The little girl no longer needs a mother.

March 13, 1984
The River House

It is now two and a half years since the spontaneous eruption of this energy. My life is externally rather limited. I do fine if nothing extra is required. Anything beyond my simple schedule produces extreme exhaustion, fire around my shoulders and neck, and familiar disaffection with myself. I have worked hard at not letting visions through, at holding back the energy. I am learning that it can be dangerous to allow them through if my body cannot withstand the impact, and yet it can also be dangerous to not allow them through. In a specific way, resistance can lead to paralysis and despair. Timing.

I come here to my bed upstairs, staring out into the whiteness, into the river, a collage of ice and stone. Tired, I lie down to rest before the children come home from school. I see.

> ❰❱ *Horses pulling*
> *covered wagons*
> *race*
> *toward me, dividing*
> *into two pathways.*
> *In this wagon*
> *adults hover*
> *around a baby*
> *a black baby*
> *in distress.*
> *She is me, kicking*
> *flailing*
> *choking.*
> *I am choking.*
>
> *One adult*
> *hangs me*
> *over the side*
> *pounding my back.*
> *A small silver ring*
> *falls out*
> *of my mouth.*
>
> *I see deep*
> *violet*
> *clouds pulsing.*

June 15, 1984
The River House

Fruits of this process become increasingly apparent. I notice that I have stopped identifying with feeling, thought, sensation in my daily life. Everything enters me, I experience it, and it leaves. Nothing stays. I am free. This quality of living is more than worth the suffering. I could have never imagined such a way. My gratitude is great. It is so good talking with Alex about this, as he understands some of what I am saying from his own experience.

Vividly, I see
animals talking
to each other
to their young.
Close up I watch
the sea otter
speaking
to its baby.

I know this.

UNION

【】

August 3–6, 1984
The River House

David and Zachary are with Nathan. I am ready to begin another retreat.
My slows increase these last few days. The vision energy is building. I
feel too tired, my body aches, the pressure behind my eyes is strong. As I
prepare to receive more visions, the deep need for a teacher returns. I
will not be seeing Alex anymore. It has become clear that he wants a
sexual relationship with me. This is devastating, crushing. He has been
the only person who seems to understand my journey because of his own
experience and thus his knowledge of this energy.

I am too tired. I do not know how to find a teacher. I learn over and
over, much to my dismay, that the master is within. I remember again:
The only way out is in and through. This transition time is difficult—I
am nowhere yet. I have left here and am not there.

[0] *I see women*
familiar
at the foot of my bed
facing me.
They kneel
except the one
directly at my feet.
She is robed
pulling her black
straight hair
into a band
at the nape of her neck.

Faceless
her robe falls away.
A fir tree
appears, painted
from her sternum
down.

Grabbing my left foot
she wraps a rope
around my big toe
pulling it off.
My foot opens
my bones revealed.

Holding both feet
she yanks them
my body undulating
many times.
She instructs me:
Sit up. Lift your
right hand.
I do so.

A nail slides
through my palm
another nail
my other palm.
Nails pierce
my ankles
my arms are pinned.

I am crucified.

Now she cuts
from the top of my leg
to the bottom
opening it
taking out the bones
putting them around
her neck
a necklace.

Cutting my other leg
she ties these bones
around her waist.

Placing my pelvic bone
on her head
for a headdress
she arranges my ribs
on her upper back
wings.

My hand bones
become her rattles.
Growing
a great clump
of tail feathers
she begins to dance.

Now she lies down
between my legs
her head hanging
over the edge
of the bed beyond
my feet.
Her words:
Hold onto my hands.
I do so, slowly.

The aching and pain in my body lessens as I receive each vision. I feel clean and calm and very tired. The pressure behind my eyes is fierce. Hannah will come soon with food. I hear the river.

[0] *Now I see her*
dancing wildly
bedecked in my bones.
I dance with her
more, more.
Merging
into one figure
multiplied by hundreds

we march
up mountains
down into valleys
arms up
decorated in feathers
dark skinned
radiant.

Hermaphroditic images are becoming constant and vivid, falling into one another. In the last twenty-four hours I have felt tremendous erotic energy, a great longing. Now such desire slowly evaporates with vision images of union. The longing for the male principle begins to be realized in my own wholeness. How strange this feels, how strange and how utterly blissful.

[0] *I see*
a vulva becoming
a phallus
becoming
a vulva.

Today I have seen the woman, the one who pulled her hair back, with a fir tree painted on her sternum, rolling with me in different positions, always with her hands on my ankles, my hands on her ankles.

[0] *Now she is a he*
lying down
at my left side
a Native American man
nursing at my breast.

Climbing on top of me
hands on ankles
he becomes also she
our heads now

yonis. With lingams
in yonis
we make a circle
somersaulting
over and melting
into aqua water
disappearing
into nowhere.

Union.

Ada comes and takes me for a walk. Back home, lying down, I listen to the river.

[O] *I see blinding*
white light
throbbing
from below
way in and down
in my yoni.

At my third eye
I see
genitals
male, female
as one
magnified, vivid.

A man
with lingam, yoni
and old white breasts
pulls his knees
up toward his chin
and slips into the water
backward.

Now I am seeing
from under the water.
I feel underwater
lying on the bottom
of a narrow tunnel
in a liminal space.

Three men swim
over the top of me
swiftly, firmly
erect.

I get into the hot water, waiting. Suddenly I feel a stronger hit of the energy, crying out as I realize I must go under the water. My hands slowly form a triangle above my genitals. With some fear and mostly awe, I let my hair loose and go under. I am told to go under on my side. As I do, my knees come up toward my chin.

◖◗ *I have a lingam*
erect
breasts and yoni.

Uncurling, I come up smoothly. Now I go under facing down, curling up again, chin to knees, then on my left side and once more on my back. The energy is terrifically strong.

◖◗ *I sit at the top*
of a very long pole
reaching
toward the infinite.
Straddling it
wearing a tiger's mask
aggressive
I am male.

155

Circles of people
way below
around the pole
wait
for me to come down.

Throwing off my mask
I slide
down to the earth
welcomed
cheered, celebrated.
The female I
with dark hair
in a female body
greets me.

We embrace
as one
male
tiger cloth around
my loins
female
naked on top.

Union.

I go to Rosalind's for dinner. She makes a tray for each of us, her delicate white dishes filled with chutney, wild rice, raisins, and sliced bananas. We bring them to the fire, light the candles, and talk about turtles, Spanish dancers, and death.

Mostly my sleep has not been disturbed this round, nor has my digestion. But last night, all night, asleep or awake, I was afraid—a flat, dark, empty fear.

【◐】 *Here I see*
me, no sex
no breasts
no yoni
no lingam
my all-white body
becomes flat
fire erupting
erupting
from the top of my head.

This last vision is so frightening to me. Hannah comes and takes me for a walk. Back into the hot water, I am tremendously afraid.

【◐】 *Trembling*
I see another
me.
The original
and white
stone, the one
with the diamond
inside, shines
at the apex
of my collarbone.

How I love it.

The image of no sexuality returns. My fingers and hands are locked in specific shapes. I cannot move them. Terrified, my body is turning to liquid. Rosa comes. She helps me get up and walk around the apartment. I am ravenously hungry. We eat crackers, cheese, and avocado sitting on the floor, leaning against the couch. With ambivalence she leaves for an appointment.

Now I wait. I am too afraid of what the coming vision will mean about my sexuality, more afraid of that than of the vision itself. I try to find Rosalind by phone. I must wait until she can be reached. I cannot see it alone. She comes now, five hours later. I see her sitting on the floor near me. Feeling protected by her presence, I open to the energy.

> **◖◗** *I see*
> *two grey breasts*
> *nipples of red light*
> *suspended above me*
> *so I can nurse.*

Each one of my hands makes a circle, with forefingers and thumbs touching. In that shape, they come before my mouth, one in front of the other. A sound comes out of my mouth, from the deepest part of me. It is very loud, complete.

> **◖◗** *More light than sound*
> *I see it*
> *evolving into mystery*
> *like a channel*
> *created by light*
> *spinning*
> *into nowhere*
> *opening*
> *wide.*

My mouth opens wider. My head is thrown back.

> **◖◗** *Now my body*
> *burns*
> *small flames*
> *reaching*
> *from every part of me*

each finger
a candle .
my body a pyre
fire carving
every edge of me.

I feel the burning
permeating
seeping, deeply entering
filling me.

I look up and see
me, the woman
taking in her arms
the sexless one
me, all white
flat, fire erupting
from the top of my head.

I see me holding
tilting the sexless body
so the fire erupting
ignites
the dark, open space
at the apex
of my collarbone.

Now that space
burns
separate, clean.
Exhilarating
that fire creates
a loop, somehow
from my neck
to the back of my eyes
out the top of my head.

Ecstasy.

Now I see
an ephemeral person
descending
on top of me
face down
long hair, breasts.

A woman
beautifully, slowly
merges
with my body
no longer burning.

Looking up, I see
a triangle, soft
in hues of pink
the very texture
of human tissue
of female tissue.

My eyes open. I am completely relieved, spent, ravenous. I can barely move, barely receive what I have just seen. I wish I didn't have to breathe. Breathing interferes.

◖◗ *I am levitating.*
I can see it
but mostly I feel it.

Ascending
welcomed
by a great male
ephemeral figure
we embrace.
Gently and freely
in this moment
he enters me.

Rolling
I spiral
horizontally down
to earth in my white
silk robe
hair falling loose.
Blissful
I arrive in the sea
swimming.

I am whole.

( ) *Full*
human size
my body is split
into two halves
right and left.

I see at my foot
a tiny and brown
unremarkable
bird
no higher
than my arch.

Slowly and growing
magnificent white
wings, gently
unevenly
it soars, carrying
a small white egg
between its feet.

Ascending
feet parting
the egg opens.

Beginning fragments
of new life
fall secretly
softly down
to earth, scattering
beyond form
beyond form.

[0] *I see Rosalind*
and me
in a small round
house, up in the dark
universe
nowhere swaying
tipping
not secure.
We glide
around the space
closing
pairs of double doors
closing them
gently.

Now my will
lowers this structure
down to the earth.
Landing in the forest
surrounded by green
the house settles.
We open the doors.
Sunlight soaks in.

We step out.

FLAMING WORLD

( )

October 24, 1984
The River House

> **[O]** *I see red*
> *deep red*
> *on my heart*
> *encircled by*
> *white.*

I feel an instinctive need to embrace the new energy by embodying a different life style. I do not want to live as I do. I feel a primitive pull, fierce, underlying everything, toward a new way. How can I learn what to choose, where to go? How will I create a life that honors what has happened?

For three weeks I have felt a fear slowly evolving, and some agitation. I have felt unwilling to sit quietly, to be alone, to listen. Today thoughts of nuclear holocaust break through. After facing this possibility, with much more clarity than before, my old struggle with the riddle of infinity reappears. It comes beyond awareness of the holocaust. I think of the recurring frightening experience (now I know it was a vision) in my early childhood in which I saw myself lying dead in a lovely child's bed, floating in the night universe, the green and brown earth visible far away and to the right. The words were: "Forever and ever and ever and ever and ever . . . "

I want to sleep. Instead I see.

> **[O]** *I see and feel*
> *an explosion*
> *from the base*
> *of my spine*
> *a white sphere*

diffusing
into white light
gently, slowly
a boom, but quiet.
In slow motion
this light fills
my entire back
jarring me.

I become light.

October 26-28, 1984
Hearthstone

Coming to the Berkshire mountains is like coming home. Theo and I ride the horses through the intensely colored hills, following the path through the woods back to High Meadow. I need this, to feel Dream's strength under me. We have a picnic lunch of salmon salad, olives, and rye bread in the sun. Theo paints. I sit by the edge of the pond, tossing pebbles, stirring the sand with a stick. I am comforted by the little leaf boats strewn across the water.

As the pressure behind my eyes begins to build, we return to the new house that Theo has just finished building. He goes back to his drawing board to continue the design work on the next house. I am alone and afraid, sitting in the small loft upstairs by the window. I hope, deeply hope, for guidance, direction. Six hours pass with only a few brief vision fragments.

[O] *I see fire*
licking upward
around the edge
of the earth.

I see a claw-like
giant machine
grabbing
crawling forward.

I see a planet
with shards of color
mostly white
in the center
slowly passing
to the left
out of sight.

I see the heel
of a human hand
pressing
into the earth
plowing across the land
forming
mountains, valleys.
I marvel
at its power
its happenstance effect.

Suddenly it is dusk. I turn and face the window. I relight the green candle, take off my diamond, and place it on the smooth sill next to the candle. My torso begins rocking in a circle as I chant. I do not know any chants or how to chant, but I am chanting as if I have been chanting for one hundred years. A long time passes, but now I definitely know more visions are coming.

[0] *An old woman*
I sit in a circle
of women
the fire burning

in the center.
I see an opening
across from me
a path
leading into the forest.

Gazing
into the fire
I realize
I am sitting
higher
than those around me.

Now I am up
very high
in a glass crucible
infused with light
limpid white light.
I sit now
as a buddha
sits.

A celestial being
appears
from above, behind
the crucible, and dives
headfirst
surfacing
up and under me
facing out.
Now in front of me
she licks a seam
where two doors
invisibly meet.
She licks
repeatedly
until they open.

Now I see the universe
the night universe.
Far, far away
I watch the world
explode
quietly, in slow motion.

The celestial being
swims
out from the crucible
toward the holocaust.
Multiplying
one by one
she measures herself
with arm's length distance
each time adding
another.

Mystical creatures
of light, of air
encircle our earth
above
holding wide
the explosion
containing it
never touching
the fire.

Now holding hands
they dive
down toward the center
of the earth
through the fire.

Two of them
here, still near me
becoming masculine

bump bellies
in metal armor
over and over
until a rod
attaches their navels.

Spinning
spinning, flipping
over the rod
they are drawn
down
into the fire
of the earth.

The energy feels too raw. I need to be in water now. But there is no water coming out of the pipes. The system is broken somewhere. Theo realizes my sense of urgency and calls Angela who is just leaving her house. She offers her bathtub and Theo drives me there immediately. I step into the hot water. Theo gets in behind me, holding me. The water touches us and space expands.

[O] *The quiet*
slow motion
explosion becomes
fire in me
electric, wild.

I see Everywoman
Everyman
their children
one by one
each, violently
whipped into the fire
of the burning earth.

The fire, red hot
burning into empty
seething space
pulls humanity
into the vortex.

I see flaming
bodies
wrapped, slapped
around the burning earth
head to toe
chains of flesh
pulled, forced into
more burning bodies
layered, molded
into the golden
black dance.

Anguished cries come out of my mouth. Theo holds me. We are in the water.

[O] *Now I see*
the burning sphere
spin
between my knees.

My hands are locked above my knees, as if holding the burning earth. My cries become chants.

[O] *I am containing*
the globe
now
as it burns.

The chants become more rhythmic, excited. I feel erotic energy building
in me with a surging vitality. Suddenly my pelvis is thrust forward and
up from the base of my spine.

> **◖◗** *Fire pours*
> *out from my yoni.*
> *Fire streams*
> *out from the apex*
> *of my collarbone.*
> *These two fires*
> *becoming one*
> *waterfall*
> *into the burning earth*
> *below me.*
> *Now this river*
> *of fire*
> *becomes a river*
> *of light*
> *white light pouring*
> *into the earth*
> *cooling the holocaust.*
> *The earth looks*
> *like a dead*
> *blackened turnip.*
>
> *I see the lingam*
> *fire burning*
> *out of the tip*
> *so lightly touching*
> *my third eye*
> *my mouth*
> *the apex*
> *of my collarbone*
> *my yoni.*

October 29–31, 1984
The River House

The children make masks with their friends. Lawrence helps. Rosa and I make an apple pie. I roll the dough for the crust, place it in the tin, and shape it to fit. Becoming too tired, I lie down on the couch. Lawrence dances by, between me and the fire, wearing an elephant mask and making strange sounds. The children dance behind him.

Rosa and Lawrence take everyone to the parade at the school. I go up to my room, feeling great relief in the whiteness of everything here. Lying down, I feel slow and quiet, no pain.

<blockquote>

[ ] *As the earth burns*
I sit
as a buddha sits
witnessing the seam
open.
The little I
stands
at the opening
bowing
to the buddha in me
asking for guidance.

Now I am Everywoman
Everyman
grabbing the seam
insisting, demanding
to shut out
the holocaust.
The doors keep
opening, refusing
to close.

Everyman

</blockquote>

leaps through
the opening, raging.
He catches himself
fingers clawing the edges
his double
hanging
across from him.

I see two men
suspended
by their fingertips
above the flaming earth
eye to eye
kicking
fighting
not letting go
swinging back
into the crucible
resting
falling again.

Now the spinning
inflamed earth
radiates
energy in concentric circles
forming a floor
touching the feet
of the men.
The energy spins
pulling them
into the fire
down and through
into the center
of the burning cauldron.

A thread spins out
from the bottom

like wool.
Fast and intense
human energy
spins into
new substance
falling
into and toward
the beyond.

The thread becomes
rope size
elongates, forming
a textured sphere
at its end.
This sphere desires
landing, hungers
to meet form.

Hanging
pulling the rope longer
falling into nowhere
the energy form
enters
the crown of the head
of a colossal figure.
Wooden and primitive
he stands.

Energy, sparks of light
shoot
out of his lingam
creating a vortex
circling down
into more vastness.

I am bent over
blackened.

I cannot see
to an end.

[O] *Now I see*
a reptile, a dragon
a lizard grown up
creeping
along the earth
fire in its eyes
and its mouth
its body made
of individuals.
Some try to get off
but magnetically
get pulled back on.

Each time this creature
opens its mouth
swallowing one being
a hundred more
appear in its tail.
One is transformed
into many.

Cruising
over mountains
into valleys
I see this giant reptile
growing wings.

I am back in the hot water, late in the day.

[O] *I see the flying dragon.*
One being dives

off of his body
into a pool
of hot water.
It is me.
My job is to see.
Our journeys are connected
the dragon's and mine.

The dragon approaches
his flame
devouring life
licking rooftops
licking doors.
People come out
being licked
being swallowed.
Licking round and round
in a circle
in the center
of a village green
the dragon licks
the center red.
The edge is white
reminiscent.

Flying
along the edge
of the earth
the dragon captures
each person
becoming
hundreds, millions
circling homes
villages, more cities
nations.

Thoughts of what to do, how to participate in the embodiment of becoming collective, becoming conscious, interfere with a flood of visions, of people moving and witnessing in continuous circles, of people awakening into clear presence.

[O] *Beyond the future*
I dive
from the crucible of light
no longer seeing
through the eye
of a buddha
landing
in the center of the earth.

The earth
burned into blackness
opens
into flat land
still hot with embers.
Beginning
with great focus
intention
I weed.

We clear.

[O] *My heart opens*
just at the place
where the diamond
pierced
my skin.
It is red, of blood.

An arrow slips
into the opening.

A man slides it out
gently, no sound
my diamond
flaming from its tip.
The man holds it
like a torch
thoughtfully walking
up Village Hill Road.

Children and animals
follow him.

December 15, 1984
The River House

I am keenly aware of the darkness this time of year, the early coming of dusk. Each day grows shorter. Each day I wait with more focus, more preparation, for the shifting of the light.

My friends have gone to hear the famous drummers in town. I am missing that. I am missing all that goes on in this world this evening. I know this in a particular way and I know that the whole world goes on inside of me, here in my room, with the river below the window, frozen and silent.

[0] *I see male genitals*
all white, clear
white.
The erect phallus
points
at my third eye
a ring of fire
spinning around it.

Energy pulses
through me
in my wrists
genitals, my neck
and beyond me
beyond me.

The male holds
me in the water
an embryo curled
on my side
between his legs.
I emerge elongated
stretched, as if
born from him.

Panicked
I see many rings
fire rings
placed one by one
on the white phallus
dominant
unchanging before my eye.
The code: one male
many females.

Thought sounds:
The new androgynous
female
must rise
to meet the androgynous
male.
Rise
to meet him.

I am she.
I cannot.

Fearful
desperately fearful
and writhing
I see
great lights
from red fire
in the hills
circling her
circling me
as she moves
as I move
as the white phallus
moves
a mating dance.

She is here.
I am here
dancing, becoming
pulsing, pulsing, fiercely
directed, flying
upward.

The energy is stunning.

EACH ONE BURNS

( )

December 28–30, 1984
Village Hill

I have come to Rosalind's for a vision retreat after the fullness of the holidays. Nathan is celebrating Christmas with David and Zachary. It is dusk. I make a fire, light the candle, take off my diamond, placing it near the candle. The house feels dark and cold. Rosalind's absence is palpable. So far, this is a very difficult retreat. There is great pressure behind my eyes but I cannot see in. Yet the energy demands form. I am afraid. I feel quite blind and very alone.

> **〔0〕** *Now I see a circle*
> *on the floor*
> *in front of me.*
> *Toy buddhas*
> *lifted by a human hand*
> *get placed one by one*
> *outside the circle*
> *eight of them.*
>
> *Emptiness.*
>
> *A small contained*
> *fire now burns*
> *in the center.*
> *A dark man*
> *stridently*
> *enters the circle*
> *placing*
> *his heel on the fire*
> *preparing*
> *to put it out.*
> *Blindfolded, removed*
> *his black footprint*
> *remains.*
>
> *Now I see eight*

thin golden lines
extending out of the fire.
Elegant, light in weight
they are the buddhas.
We are all alive.
I am this one
facing the fire.

The one to my left
looms larger, more golden
elevated
the others softer
becoming more human
their arms wrapped
in white muslin
leaving
their hands free
to cup upward.

Each buddha
leans
far forward, toward
the center fire
flanked by pairs
of hands
offering.

I see these hands
close up
in shades of gold
human hands
holding nothing
waiting, waiting.

One right hand
examined gently
by the man
with the diamond torch

reveals a hole
bloody
in the palm.

The blood, traveling
for generations
marks pathways
toward the center
where the hand has been pierced.
The man
licking the wound
slowly wraps
the hand in white muslin.

Death? White
appears high above
to the left
beyond an edifice
an ancient stone structure.

At the top
I see
an angelic being
crawling
through a space
trying to follow
the emptiness.

The man keeps licking
the wound.

I awaken all night at five minutes after each hour. No fear. I wait for dawn. I get into the hot water. The energy is instantly strong and active.

◖◗ *I see the pairs*
of hands, palms up

around a central fire
burning in a copper cup.
A larger hand
drops
a spark of fire
into the palm
of each hand
burning
right through. Hands
are wounded
all hands, all people.

I feel sudden pain in a specific spot on my spine.

(Ⓘ) *Another cup of fire*
enters my spine
midway
burning upward
stopping
at the back of my neck
settling
at the base of my vocal chords.

Hands stacked
on top of it
the fire burns
a clean hole through each
leaving
a left hand on top.

All palms face upward.

I feel tormented and despairing. It is too difficult to let in this energy.
Suddenly my voice opens and sounds come out with a resonance, depth,
and clarity that are unknown to me. This voice can go way down,

across to either side, or up. I see its course as if mapped, as visual as it is aural. This place is far beyond me yet coming through me. I feel frightened by the power of the voice. I weep, call, ache, and struggle. I want someone to come. No one comes.

(0) *The man with the torch*
kneels
next to the tub
taking my right hand
licking the wound.

Now I take that hand so slowly and with the other hand as agent, immerse it in the water. As I do so I hear myself shouting: "For all men, women, and children." That right hand moves up the inside of my left arm to my left breast. It holds the breast, offers it. My left palm touches the nipple, comes to my mouth, is made wet there, and goes out toward all the people I see. Now both hands go up slowly, throbbing and hot.

(0) *Each hand*
ringed in light
glows.

How can I do this? I am ravaged, exhausted. Throughout this entire time, especially in the water, my hands are very active, making a whole by touching each other in some way. Now they come together to form a circle, forefinger to forefinger and thumb to thumb, beyond my third eye. I sense what I might see in that space is too great, too much to be able to see.

(0) *Blue*
now white light
I cannot stay.

The pressure builds again.

[O] *I sit*
in the circle
in the forest again
where the nuclear
holocaust
visions began.
A row of people
looking like pilgrims
file into the round.
They keep coming
shaping circle after circle
hundreds, thousands
looking up at me.

I realize what they ask:
What is it?
What will happen?

I hear my voice:
It is TERRIBLE.
I do not know
what I speak about.

I begin to cry.
I see Shona
to my left in the road
badly burned
only bones and muscle
remain.
She reaches for help
or is she giving up?
Now I see another
girl, rolling toward me
hysterical
on fire.

I see her terror
her pain.

It is TERRIBLE.

I see others
who I know
who I love
burning
one by one.

Devastation.

Always, at some level, the energy itself protects me, regardless of content. Now, for the first time, I feel unprotected while I am seeing.

[O] *I see*
David and Zachary
throwing themselves
toward me
flaming.

Wrapping us
all three
in the bear blanket
we fall
into nowhere
no end
to our slow fall
into vaporous spirals
turning.

I see more people
running toward me
frantic
on the road
wearing black
masks of cloth
material flowing behind
flaming.

A great mechanical
monster
sprays life with fire.
Now I see
the firing machine
stop
running out of power.

Hands hurl
bodies
burning
piling them in a heap
one by one
everyone
I love most.
I see
David and Zachary
on the top.

I am slipping under, without protection, screaming.

[○] *I watch our sons*
burn
part by part
bare feet
legs
genitals
hearts
hands and faces.

I find my hands
over the pile
of burning people
over our sons
blessing them

as the fire rages
blessing them.

Souls don't burn.

This vision, the destruction of the individual, is unbearable. What I see
has happened in the past, happens now in the present somewhere, and
will again happen in the future. I feel exhausted, drained, alone. My
eyes burn with pressure and pain.

It is early afternoon. The hours move through me. I realize with great
difficulty that I have more to see. I need someone to come. I am losing
faith in the purpose, the power, the gift of this process. As I lie here
during these long hours, my hands keep turning so that the palms are
up,

[0] *spikes nailed*
through the holes
in my palms.

I move less, feel numb, blank. At the deepest level, I know I must wait
until dusk, until I can get back into the water. This feels austere and
correct. I am barely hanging on. I am mostly out of my body, unable to
keep my eyes open. I move very slowly, blindly, and with great difficulty.
Hannah comes with Jeanette and Julia. I feel self-conscious about the
two women seeing me like this. I cannot let myself attach to that fear. I
will die if I waver from my efforts to focus utterly on what is happening
in my body.

I get into the water. I feel possessed, entered by a force fuller than I can
organize in my body. My hands and mouth especially hold it. Two
screams soar out of me, two screams. My hands are making specific
shapes at the corners of my mouth. I see a myriad of images of those I
love burning, and cascades of pulsing white and blue lights. My left hand,
after slowly being touched by my right hand in the center of the palm, is

[0] pulled to the wall
nailed to the wall.

My right hand, after being touched in the center of the palm by my
tongue, is pulled to the other wall.

[0] Pulled, nailed
the nails are black
iron, immense.

I cry out.

[0] There is no way
to get down.

Time passes. I hear myself calling David and Zachary.

[0] My sons come to me
in sweatshirts
jeans.
Zachary gently
directly
looking so little
so sure
takes my right hand
off of the nail.
David, open
transparent
intently
takes my left hand
off of the nail.
Slowly, now
my hands on their heads
and I bless them.

We laugh
the three of us
when we realize
we are standing
in water.

(●) *Hundreds of people*
slightly bow
to someone.
Each wears black
over their heads
shoulders
backs.
I see them
from the left side.

Too afraid
I stop seeing.

I feel the same uneasiness and apprehension I felt in another vision, in the first months, when thousands of people were waiting for someone to appear before them. I know who it is. My fingers make a circle. Rocking, I look through it with my third eye. The energy is now beyond any hope of my surviving it. May I be able to see what I am ready to see.

I cannot describe what I see. Arching backward, I take my left foot up into my right hand, creating a circle. The circle embodied, the energy is now contained. I hold the burning individuals with an energy infinitely greater than me. I am clear now. Finally the strength with which to hold the destruction and destructiveness of the individual has moved into and through me.

I am too exhausted, empty, so glad it is over. How will I ever get back from this round? I am so grateful that Hannah is with me.

SUFFERING WORLD

【】

January 7–8, 1985
The River House

I have recently been given a very old green glass bracelet that I love. An empty circle, it is potent. I lay it on my altar near my diamond. Lighting the candle, I burn sage and place my stones exactly where they must be in relationship to me and the fire. I know now that the fire is sacred.

> **[ ]** *I see a dead swan*
> *sacrificed*
> *insides exposed*
> *on this altar.*
> *The long neck*
> *pushed down into my neck*
> *head in my mouth*
> *the bill between my lips*
> *fills me.*
> *It makes me sit*
> *upright.*
>
> *Is there something*
> *small, red*
> *inside the neck*
> *of the swan?*
>
> *Blood.*

Chanting, energy building in my body, my arms, hands, and mouth are moving. I hold my feet, bare feet. May I be able to see what I am ready to see. Suddenly, my hands literally take hold of something,

> **[ ]** *a swan's neck.*
> *I slowly squeeze*
> *choking him*
> *breaking his neck*

hearing the loud sound
the snap.

I go to the bathroom with the candle and get into the hot water.

[O] *I feel fire*
below
far below.
The man with the torch
appears
close up
getting into my mouth
with his hands
pulling out
numerous flags
from my throat.
He pulls out
the white stone
but it is cloth now
surrounding the diamond.

He drops the diamond
into my ear.
I feel it
I see it falling
into my throat.

I come back to the fire in the living room, drained of all energy, surrendering to a terrible weight. My hands make specific shapes that are sustained for long periods of time. Now I see.

[O] *My left hand*
holds my right arm
up a little.

My right hand cut off
my left hand cut off
these hands
no longer mine
form a circle
up and out
from my third eye.

I look up, into and through the circle.

[0] *I encounter*
a loop of light
ablaze
my third eye on this side
one eye
or two on the other.
Fire burns
through the center
clearing it.

I realize that the green glass bracelet is my first form, first tool. I can look through it. It is a shape, a window that stands between this world and the other worlds. I can use my will in relationship to this form. I feel elated realizing this. I sing, chanting a song of gratitude. It is the sound of good spirit. I like it.

Now, early in the morning, it is still dark, just before dawn. I climb into the steaming water. It is quiet, peaceful. Mostly, I see clear empty nothing.

[0] *The man enters me*
his lingam receiving
the diamond
that fell from my ear

into my throat
down
into the center of me.
The diamond
moves into his lingam
traveling up
and into his mouth.

Kissing me
passing the diamond
into my mouth
it is now spilling
into my throat
down my center
into his lingam
in me
in stillness.

This loop
repeating itself
over and over
engraves a heart.
The path, smooth
the diamond path
vividly etched
becomes
a loop of light
created by male and female
bodies.

A union.

I see
the diamond heart
energy
moving
the other way

through his lingam
into my yoni
up into my throat
from my mouth to his
a kiss ·
down his throat
torso
into his lingam
back into me
in stillness.

Either way.

March 8–10, 1985
The River House

Theo has left for Morroco to paint. He is traveling and too far away to be in touch by mail. Speaking to him on the phone today reminds me that physical distance becomes less significant to me somehow. I know him wherever he is.

There continues to be a band of energy through which I usually have to move before I can receive the visions. In that place, I am filled first with emotion—sadness, fear, confusion, loneliness. Then I weep more fully, feeling such despair about our world. And then somehow I feel as though I am out on the other side of an edge on which I am directly experiencing infinite time and space. The visions exist there. All of this paradoxically occurs within me. Sometimes, coming out of the visionary state, I again pass through these specific spaces of sensation.

I sit legs crossed, facing the fire. There are two candles. I lean against the couch, the white pillow at my back. Slowly I sink into where I really am. The energy fills me.

◖◗ *David walks toward me*
hands as if in prayer
bowing
leaving to the left.
I sit as the buddha
nature in me
hands as if in prayer
bowing to David.

Zachary walks toward me
hands as if in prayer
bowing
leaving to the right.
I sit as the buddha
nature in me
hands as if in prayer
bowing to Zachary.

Suddenly
the two boys meet
embracing, laughing.

Others come toward me
one by one
saying goodbye
bowing.
I bow.

It is as though I call them here to say goodbye so that who they are and what they represent can leave my consciousness as I prepare to be in another realm.

◖◗ *I see me*
Janet Adler
walking

toward me.
She reads a paper
to university students.
Undressing
now naked
she stands
before me.

I cry as I watch her
relieve herself
of feces, urine
menstrual blood.
Emptied, naked
she is just a person
just a person.
She climbs into my lap.

Embracing her
profoundly moved
I see
a purple candle
quietly burn
a large hole in the center
of her paper.

She stands
before a flesh-colored
opening
to a dark passageway.
A man in a bright red
turban, smiling
with open face
welcomes her.

I have seen him before.

Janet, on all fours
reduced
to her animal nature
barks like a dog.
Golden talons
grab her, pulling
her into the tunnel.
He holds her
his back to
the buddha nature in me.
The tunnel is dark
some water on the ground
some light
at the other end.
The doors to the tunnel
close. My mind
opens them
but they are at once
closed.

I am to wait
to sleep. I do so.

My back hurts. I am very much in my slows. The infusion of energy is intense. I can barely move. I am one piece of intense matter.

【◎】 *Emerging from the tunnel*
he carries Janet
and stands her up.
Gradually, beginning
with her feet
she becomes invisible.
She is there.
I sense her energy

but I cannot see her body.
I see her energy.

By the time she moves
to her left
facing me
I see nothing.
She in her old form
disappears
her essence
somersaulting
into my lap
becoming one
with the buddha
nature in me.

A union.

Dusk finally arrives. I light the candle, feeling weepy. The light and the quiet are exquisite and foreboding. I go into the water for the changing of the light.

[O] *I see infinite*
numbers of people
coming toward me
each suffering.
I touch a young
blond girl
enduring the curve
of a large needle
jabbing into her navel
out her yoni.
She is in agony
each one behind her
in agony.
There are thousands.

I see each one
each one's uniqueness.

May I learn
to help.

I am restless and distracted in the water. So what? I weary of taking this all so seriously. Unconsciously, I offer my left breast.

◖◗ *A command:*
No more being sucked on
no more sucking.

Later, again without thinking or noticing, unconsciously, I offer my right breast.

◖◗ *Again:*
No more being sucked on
no more sucking.

Now bending over
I sit in sand
rubbing it on my
hands, arms
mixing it with water
smearing mud
on my body.

The woman
of the white hands
brings
the suffering
people, one by one
to sit in a circle
in front of me.

I feel restless, distracted, embarrassed. I realize I am avoiding this vision. May I be able to see what I am ready to see.

[O] *I begin to draw*
in the sand
with my finger.
The first person
comes to me
lying down on a mat
in front of me
face down.

I chop her body
in half
with the edge
of my right hand
now gently pushing
the two halves
apart.

Creating a shape
in front of me
I push the sand
together with both hands
leaving an opening
at the top.

I am increasingly distracted. I do not know what to do. May I be able to see what I am ready to see.

[O] *People sit in pain*
in great need
one by one
the circle filling.

My helplessness
mounts.

There is no one here with me. I fear this intensity with no other person here to help ground it. I get out of the water. I sleep with the thickness of the energy all night, awakening into a very heightened state. The only relief is to see.

[0] *I see me*
the union
of the buddha nature in me
and Janet
sitting at the head of the circle
of suffering people.

I see the shape
in the sand
a rising-up place.
The opening reminds me
of the white stone
with onyx lips
black and shining.

Now I see into
water below
an exquisite place
delicate somehow
with great light
glowing
around it.

Dipping my hand
into the numinous
I sprinkle
this wetness

onto the broken
body
before me.

I weep as I realize what I am doing. I feel embarrassed and scared. The energy builds, my breathing changes. I feel pain and tremendous agitation.

[O] *I dip*
into the water
with my right hand
showering
my left arm
with the blue
shimmering fluid.
Seduced
I try to step in
all of me
lowering myself
into this pool.

I hear a loud
emphatic NO.

I can barely contain the energy. I try to walk around the house. It is very difficult. I pass the magnificent red tulips under the window. Weeping, I can barely move. I lie down. I want to be held, touched. I feel erotic energy.

[O] *I see a man*
on the edge of the circle
to my right
kneeling
legs apart.

His sperm is abundant
radiating
out, into the circle
onto the body
of the broken girl.
The semen
seals the seam
where she is split.

Opening my legs
marking a specific design
with my fingers
I spread
my menstrual blood
along the edges
of the seam.

I see cuts
between her breasts
over her heart.
Semen and blood
mend the wounds
more on each eyelid
between her toes.

Two black men
lift her
carrying her
around the inside
of the circle.
Months pass.

Sitting up
on one man's shoulders
she jumps down
whole again.

I am too weak. Suddenly I am starving. I eat an apple and some crackers and now fall into another dense sleep. Hannah comes when dusk arrives. We light the candles. I place some white yarn in a circle on the floor in front of the fire, place the green glass bracelet at the top, and sit at the bottom. A ritual is developing that I like. It feels correct.

I cut off
each hand
with the other.
Those hands lift
the glass circle
up until
it contains the vision space.

I look
into this circle
seeing a pool
of clear water.
The suffering people
all come toward me.
The woman
of the white hands
brings them
one by one.

This man, very old
bald, with a long
white beard, sits
on the edge
of the pool.
The woman
of the white hands
lowers him
so small,
into the water.

His words in me:
I am ready to die.

Floating down
the middle of the pool
climbing onto my left thigh
he is dead
the size of my thumb.
I feel open, present
as I receive him.

This woman comes
with no life
in her lower half
short, light hair
of stocky build.
The woman
of the white hands
helps her into
the water.
She swims vigorously
with her arms.
I witness.

Now a baby
in a basket
with an inflamed rash
now a boy
badly burned
his heart opening
in the water.
Others
each suffering
one by one
slip into the water.

I sit
in their presence
feeling whole
clear.

I am the buddha nature
in me, sitting
before a pool of water
multiplying into hundreds
of buddhas
before hundreds of pools
full
of hundreds
of suffering people.

Sitting up, I straighten my legs and pull a long imaginary thread from between my knees, hand over hand.

[ ] *The needle*
in my right hand
enters
my third eye
moving out the other side
behind me
and down
back into my heart
out the front of me
and up
to the next person
slightly above me.

Looking down to my left
I see endless people
threaded this way
looking up to my right

endless more
looming larger.

An exquisite and unusually powerful image, born directly out of specific movement in my body. I begin to draw this configuration on the rug because I want it whole. I want these threads to create a complete circle and they never do, of course, because there is always a new individual, a new configuration. I am greatly relieved to more directly experience my relationship to the suffering in the world.

Suddenly the energy sweeps back into me with great power. My breathing changes. I need to be in the hot water, but I am so slow. I give Hannah my diamond to hold.

() *Peace*
for a long time
and I become smaller
smaller, bowing
to a great buddha
with endless
increasingly larger
buddhas
behind him.
All of the suffering people
come toward me
in shadow.
I sit, large
as a buddha sits
in shadow.

They come
from the opening
in the forest
quickly
single file

through my body
heart level.
My center pulses
as they move
through me
through my opening
into infinity.

I feel profoundly sad. I sit at the top of the steps, sobbing. I see the light through the prism dancing above me and think of Rilke: "Only the song above the land blesses and celebrates." I see the white door at the bottom of the steps. I see the raincoats, snow pants, mittens, hats. I see the walking staff. It is all there to support me, to protect me when it is difficult outside. All I have to do is open the door and go out into the world and try to help. But today I am sitting at the top of the steps, weeping.

DIALOGUE
【】

March 29-30, 1985
The River House

For a week the energy has been coming back. I did not realize what was happening since I never expected another round so soon after the last one. My digestion is significantly slowed down, my sleep consistently disrupted. There is fire in my back and much pressure behind my eyes. David and Zachary are with Nathan for another spring vacation.

Today the pressure is building so fast that neither sleeping nor meditation helps, nor does the river or lying on the earth under a circle of birch trees at Village Hill. I clean the house in preparation. Rosa will be here soon.

In the meantime I must walk. My way of perceiving is unusual. As I walk outside, trees, houses, cars look ever so slightly liquid. As I sit by the river, the rocks move. My left eye is noticeably larger. I experience frequent heart quickening.

Now by the fire indoors, the energy is insistent and the pressure behind my eyes intense. I feel afraid of what I am going to see—not of the vision itself, but of what it might mean in my life. I get into the water and feel the violence of the energy, raw and racking. I struggle terribly and move too much, all from impulse. Rosa arrives. The energy grows absolutely fierce. I want desperately to stay in my body, contain what is coming. I feel, as I did last night, that I might die. I am compelled to put my head under three times. The third time I feel the surge of the energy, a brief moment of ecstasy, and fully immerse myself in the water. Now I can see.

> [O] *For a split second*
> *I glimpse*
> *a divine force.*

My left foot seems enormous. Rosa helps me out of the water, wrapping me warmly in the softness of the towel. She says my experience reminds her of labor contractions. On the couch, the energy starts to build again, fast. Ada arrives with a gardenia. I think of Mother, her love for that flower. The energy is building so fast I stand up in a state of emergency, though my movement is unbearably slow. I place the white yarn circle on the floor by the fire. Ada is on my left and Rosa is on my right.

Now I feel my body fill with fire, but it is white fire, white light. It does not any longer burn or bring pain. It feels like the quickening in my heart, but radiating throughout within me, this time vibrating up and out of my throat and mouth. It is strangely pleasurable, soothing.

> **[ ]** *I see*
> *a semblance*
> *of the face again.*
> *First I see*
> *one eye*
> *a left eye*
> *slightly below*
> *the full face*
> *that I see*
> *almost immediately*
> *after seeing*
> *the eye.*
> *It is a white face*
> *indescribable.*

A divine force—I saw it once before, on a cold Thanksgiving day, very briefly, in the hot water, when I saw a body become a diamond body. How strange . . . with no belief in a personal God, a God with will or intention, I am seeing now the God that I imagined as a small child. Perhaps the presence of this God offers a primitive form, a metaphor from my own Western roots. Why, I wonder. Does this form help me to contain or to embody this energy?

❮❯ *He tells me*
to listen.

My right ear feels huge and hot. I am sitting in the center of the white yarn circle made on the floor, my arms up, elbows bent, my hands in fists. I do not see this. I am doing it.

❮❯ *He demands:*
Open your fists.
I see and hear him
above me
slightly to my right.

I try as hard as I can to do what he says, but I cannot breathe and it is taking too long. It is taking all of me to open my fists. I do so finally. They are open. I fall back with my arms straight out to my side, all of my energy spent.

❮❯ *With a light touch*
with no pain
no fight
my hands are nailed
to a cross.
Now he commands
again with power
and directness
that overwhelm me:
Straighten your legs.

I do this more easily, though it takes time.

❮❯ *My feet are nailed*
to a cross.

I feel light and clear now, as if it is all over. There is no more pain, but the energy is vividly present. As I realize that I am now crucified, I plead for whatever comes next to be the last exchange. I touch the soles of both my feet, the center where the nails are. I do the same with the palms of my hands, then lick them, the way the man with the torch does. Eventually I fall down backward. I curl up into a ball. I cannot do more.

[○] *One word*
in empty space:
Communion.

I resist, feel shy, feel as though I cannot. A nice Jewish girl from Indiana, I know little of these Christian rituals. Forcing myself and with much difficulty, I stand up and try to walk to the kitchen. Ada and Rosa hold me up, one on each side. In the refrigerator I find bread, wine, and the two little baskets of three hard-boiled eggs each that I prepared yesterday, not knowing why.

Now it is clear that I am conducting a communion ritual, with Ada on my left and Rosa on my right, as if I know what I am doing. We eat ceremoniously, and my last gesture is a blessing over the eggs. I am completely exhausted. All afternoon, I am restless, unable to sleep. Talking with Ada, sitting on the outside steps in too much light, I feel great stomach pain. I am so thankful she will stay with me tonight.

At dusk I prepare the space.

[○] *I see*
a great swan
coming toward me.
Something is wrong.
Crooked
not perfect
pausing
she drinks in the pool

in front of me.
I whisper:
Your neck is broken.

In absolute horror
I realize
it is I
who broke her neck
long ago
at the altar.
She nods in agreement.
I plead:
I am sorry.
I had to.
I was told to.
I did not mean to.
I just had to do it.

Panicked, I realize
I am Everywoman
Everyman
wounding another.
No way back.
I wonder
about forgiveness.

She keeps drinking.

Now I see a waterfall
plunging
into an apricot
ocean, the fall
on my right
the ocean on my left.

I feel frustrated and experience an abortive attempt to communicate with the divine force. Finally, both arms go out to my sides like in a crucifixion, but this time they are limp.

[O] *I hear him again*
insisting
I put my legs out
in front of me.
He keeps asking:

Do you remember?

Do you remember
your suffering?

Do you remember?

In slow motion and without emotion, I am being moved. My right hand comes over the side of my face, as though I have been hit.

[O] *Do you remember*
hitting
and being hit?

My fingers touch each eye.

[O] *Do you remember*
blinding
and being blind?

My hands move down across my face and neck to my heart.

[O] *Do you remember*
stabbing
and being stabbed?

My hands gesture as though they are cutting off my legs.

[(0)] *Do you remember*
maiming
and being maimed?
Each time
his voice
loud and clear:

Do you remember?
Never forget.

I pull the white yarn circle around me, pulling my legs into a bent position. The yarn becomes tangled. Very slowly I untangle it.

[(0)] *I hear him:*
Now you are free.

I pull the yarn together and push it through the glass bracelet. In doing so, I say goodbye to a specific sense of suffering I have always known within me. I lift the bracelet up with my right hand.

[(0)] *He asks:*
Can you see me now?
I see his eye
with my left eye
directly
on the other side.

One more person free
this time
my turn.

I am thankful
profoundly thankful.

RETURNING

【】

March 31–April 2, 1985
The River House

I awaken feeling very uneasy with heart quickenings since 5:00 A.M.
They fill my body. The white fire is present again, but this morning it is
so unsettling. I cannot sense where I am in this cycle—the rhythm feels
different. I go downstairs. I want an open fire. Looking at it is the first
sense I have today of being on track. Without much thought I sit on the
cushion facing the fire, and hold a big, egg-shaped stone from Ada that
just happens to be on the floor nearby. I see an image that is now
familiar, recurrent.

> ◖◗ *One eye*
> *close up*
> *an eye of a bird*
> *looks at me*
> *blinking.*

I am compelled to bend over into a ball on my knees. This feels exactly
right. Weeping, my hair falls over beyond my head onto the floor. I
divide it. Two halves make a V.

> ◖◗ *I see an arc*
> *between the two halves*
> *as my left forefinger*
> *draws it.*
> *Now I see an egg*
> *suspended on the arc*
> *in my hair.*
>
> *With my third eye*
> *I see a white egg*
> *balancing*
> *on burning logs*

in a fire
a brilliant vision.

I begin to weep
never stopping.
I cup my hands
together, into a shape
placing this shape
near the top
of my head.
I see
the diamond inside.

Blowing
down into my chest
under my sweater
my hands cup
further away from my head
closer to the fire
suspended there
a long time.
The diamond becomes
an egg in my hands.

Three eggs now
one in my hair
one in the fire
one in my hands.
Still weeping, I wonder
which egg
marks the source.

They are the same
burning
burning
through the fire
into my hands.

This is why I cry.
The fire sears
my hands.

Slowly I lie down. Curled up under the bear blanket, my hair covers my face. I hold the black stone egg. I am waiting.

⬭ *I ask how long*
must I wait.
Clearly:
Forty days and forty nights.

Exhausted but very awake, I hear the fire crackling softly and the washing machine washing the clothes. The floor shakes on the spinning cycle. How long do I really wait? I want to stretch, kick, elongate. I go to the kitchen and get a real, white egg. Coming back to the fire, I carefully place the egg on the burning logs. This is a most exquisite image in all ways.

The egg is slightly off-center toward the left, balanced on two logs, facing right. The egg roasts, now burns. Yellow oozes out. This is the blood. A transparent bubble appears at the larger end. This is the soul. The egg is hatching new life, free, without form. Slowly the shell, now empty, begins to burn until it too looks like a charred log. Ada says it looks like a phoenix preparing to take flight. The bottom third is all that is left. It is black, delicately formed, secure on the log, a container for new life. Rebirth through fire. It is an ecstatic time, seeing the egg in the fire. I cannot write anymore. Writing hurts my arm. Suddenly I realize if I do not record this, Ada will somehow. Is my turn finished? Is she next? We are each initiates, one by one.

Dusk has come. How I wait for it. There is pressure behind my eyes, but otherwise all is quiet.

RETURNING

[O] *I see at once*
a diamond
my diamond
on its chain.
It is large now
hanging around
a neck.
I can only see
the collarbone
the shoulders
of a man, a giant man.
The face
I cannot see.

Now I see
a golden ball
the sun, coming in
from the left
landing
on the third eye
of the buddha.
The buddha wears
the diamond.

Drops of fire
descend
into a purple abyss
reaching the vortex
and coming up again
slowly, poignantly
becoming
a purple heart.

[O] *I see people in black robes*
moving back

praying
touching
a bas-relief stone
sculpture of Jesus
on the cross.

An old man crawls
out of the crowd
trying to touch
him.
It is cold as people
turn, a quarter turn
touching this god
who becomes a skeleton
turning again a quarter
turn, touching this god
who becomes a wooden statue
turning again
a quarter turn
touching this god
who becomes
a metal stoplight.

The old man
peels back the red, the green
peeling through
to a face
discovering underneath
a spinning diamond
its point balancing
at the center
of a surrendered tulip
white.

This night Hannah takes me to hear the Tibetan monks. I feel very strange and self-conscious in such a public place. There are too many people here for me. Hannah leaves my side for a second and I feel painfully vulnerable. The chanting affects me strongly—great fire in my back, heart quickening, many visions. This last one is completely indescribable.

(() *I see*
a clear white sphere
of light
passing from monk
to monk
illuminated
radiating from
a central force
a God, a Buddha
enlightening
the whole world.

I awaken this morning feeling terrible—bad stomach pains, unease, tears. The energy is exceptionally strong again, creating great difficulty. I miss Theo so. He will be back soon from Morocco. I step into the water.

(() *I see me*
in this white tub
ascend into the heavens.
Simultaneously I see
me, here in this tub
on earth.
As I enter the deep
heavens, two stars
one at a time
come toward me
skimming the water
around me

returning to their places
in the sky.

Now a white bird
of light
circles the white tub
with me inside
shaping
the tub into a perfectly
round, open
pool of water.
The white yarn
looping around the pool
begins moving
creating a link
toward the tub
on earth.

I am braiding
the yarn
white, purple, red
becoming all white.
Wearing white
slowly braiding
I move
downward.

I see celestial
beings, they are eleven
on alternate sides
of the white-silver cord
a myriad of silver threads
woven together.
Each being places
a hand on opposite
sides of the braid.

I cannot see this braiding continue. I cannot. The energy builds. My thumb touches my mouth. My forefinger touches my forehead, my third eye.

> **[0]** *My mouth, marked*
> *the medium*
> *between energy*
> *and form*
> *words*
> *talking, writing*
> *touching this world.*
>
> *My third eye, marked*
> *the medium*
> *between light*
> *and this body*
> *a source*
> *a touch from the other worlds.*
>
> *They must work together.*

This suprises me somehow. My life before these recent years of total immersion in the numinous was replete with expressive movement in response to the texture of my world. My creative energy always found form through dance. And I often discovered form through deeply satisfying work with clay. Now it is obvious to me that words become the form that best reflect my initiation experience, not choreography, not sculpture. Intuition and clear thinking are becoming the same. This union can be voiced in writing or speaking. The way opens directly, from body to word.

I call Hannah. She is here now, kneeling next to the tub. I place my left thumb on her mouth, my forefinger on her third eye. Now placing both of my thumbs together, I dip them three times, then dip the forefingers together three times into the water.

(●) *Now Hannah and I*
meet
in the middle
between the two worlds
straddling the braid.
She slides down
I slide
up, she slides up
and I slide down.
Riding the silver threads
my twin and I
up and down
embracing
down and up
embracing again
until we disappear.

Holding my feet in the water I feel whole, relieved.

(●) *The man with the torch*
stands guarding
the pool in the heavens.
Theo stands, guarding
the white tub on earth.

The Tibetan monks
chant in a circle
holding it all.
The celestial beings
float along the silver line.
I sit whole
in both waters.

It is midafternoon. Nancy comes with chicken soup. I take off my red
socks, thinking that they are the color of blood, placing them in a

particular way on the floor. I put the glass bracelet at the top. I hold my feet. I feel many simple intuitive directions regarding the placement of my hands. The energy is a fierce undertow. I am sinking.

[0] *I see his eye*
and hear him ask:
Do you know
I am here?
My arms lifting
up, straight up
above my head
energy pouring through me
ascending, I descend
white candles burning
on each side of me
marking a path.

My arms lowering
one-third of the way
down
my breath ceases.

Ecstasy.

My arms float
down another third
still no breath.

Elation.

Gliding
now landing
on this earth
in utter stillness
I am weightless.

Exquisite.

Intuitively I know that it is time now to make an offering of gratitude for this entire journey, my initiation. My hands cup, but I still do not know what to put in them. I wait, hoping to see what to offer. I think of everything that has value to me. I think of my stone, the glass bracelet, a butterfly. I notice that my head is slightly bent forward and I am unbraiding my hair, undoing the one big braid.

Hannah comes back at dusk. The fire in my back is fierce. With much sadness, exhaustion, and pain, I open myself by taking the glass bracelet into my hands. I throw my head and hair forward as I bend over my knees onto the white rug in front of the fire. I begin to weep. I feel such sadness and loss as I enmesh the glass circle in the thickness of my hair. It is my hair that I am offering.

I put all of my hair through the glass circle. The question is, how much? I make a fist with my left hand around the ends of my hair. The bracelet lies on top of the fist. I push it up with my right hand, making another fist on top of the first one. I do this up to four fists. I stop back at two fists. That is how much. I have not cut my hair since the initiation began. It has become much fuller, longer, and wild in these five years.

This morning I awaken very unsettled, agitated, my heart quickening. Death is with me constantly. I come downstairs, light the candles, and lie on the floor. Hannah is coming soon. I cannot wait. I pick up the phone, find the number that Lawrence gave me for a famous authority on this energy, and call him. I cannot believe I am doing this and I cannot believe that he answers. I try to briefly and clearly explain what is happening. I tell him that I am dying. He tells me to go ahead and die, implying it is only metaphor. I try to explain that metaphor exists in the content of the visions, but my real body is dying now. I do not know what I expect him to say, but I wonder why he would make such a suggestion, especially in the context of a brief phone conversation. I feel completely misunderstood and so alone again. I remember: The master is within. I climb into the hot bath.

RETURNING

【0】 Theo faces me
in the water
speaking lovingly.
I hear him
so clearly.

As he moves
behind me
supporting me
I see a spiral
from before
the beginning
dark, black
burning through
my life, perhaps
my lives
evolving into now.
At this end I see
a little black box.

Theo smooths
rounds the edges
into a white egg.
Tying rope
around it, swinging it
over his head
a lasso
hurling it
into space
it opens
opens, multiplying
into openings
lights
released into the universe.

One form, the bottom third
of the egg

233

like the roasted egg
remains
a place in the midst
of the infinite
array of light.

The energy builds. I keep inhaling deeply and blowing out. I hear myself knocking with the back of my hands on the sides of the tub. Eleven times, eleven times, and eleven more. I hear my sounds, sobs. I feel so terribly afraid.

[0] *I see the circle*
of monks, the silver
braid, the two tubs.
I see again
his face.
He asks:
Do you see me?
I do.

I see a white
egret
slowly appearing
before me
facing west
her cape, a butterfly
of irridescent stars.
She tells me:
I give you this cape
a gift from him.

Humbled
grateful without words
trying
to simply receive it
I will gladly

cut my hair, gladly
let go, gladly die.

I can barely move, talk, walk, see. I hear the river. Real physical death
is now so possible. Surprisingly void of emotion, I simply do not have
the strength to stay in my body. I focus completely on my boys and my
promise to myself to survive this energy because I am their mother.
Lawrence is here trying to help me hang on. Brian sits nearby. I can see
his long white beard. Nancy tries to get me to crawl on the floor where
I might feel more grounded. I hear Zach's footsteps in his cowboy boots
on the stairs coming up to my loft. He gives me his giant drawing of a
lion, so clearly formed, so powerful. Courage is what I need.

I can only feel life in the strip of pain across my shoulders.

I see his hand
slowly reaching
taking the cape of heaven
off the egret
reaching
toward me
laying it down
upon my shoulders
where white feathers
grow.

I am leaving my body.

Not deciding to resist, not knowing to scream, I scream from the center
of my being, screaming "NO! NO!" to whatever force is literally taking
me out of my life.

[ ] *The cape of butterfly*
of blue, of stars

I will not
receive it.
Egret, take it back
take it back
into spirit
without me!
I return
into my body.

I am alive.

I get into the hot water, slowly opening my eyes. I see the reflection of the candle flame in the water burning exactly over my yoni, the small gentle flame where it was when all of this began, down at the base of my spine. I see it reflected there in the water and simultaneously I feel it, the white light, no more burning, just white flame throughout my body. I find my hand on my heart. This is what the flame has done. It has opened my heart.

It is near noon. All morning I have been alone. Now I am breathing heavily, feeling suspended. I know the universe is impeccably ordered. I know this. The energy has taught me. It is 11:30. I find the white silk cloth, the grey silk cloth, and the beige silk cloth. I lock all the doors. May I be able to do what I am ready to do. I cut two fists high off of my hair with two long, slow cuts, one on each side. Smiling, I feel immediate relief.

I place the two fists full of hair together and wrap grey cord around the bunch. I lay it in the white and grey silk, wrapping it with rust cord. It feels as though something dead is inside. It looks like something prepared for burial. I will bury it on Rosalind's land next to the Quonset hut. I braid a small clump that I left out and roll it in the beige silk. I will take this braid to the river. I feel encased in a sacred sphere.

At dusk I go to Rosalind's land. There is a place to the left of the stone steps in front of the hut. I dig a deep hole and place the bundle of hair in it. I fill the hole, gathering the soil with my hands. The earth feels wonderful—wet and cold. It smells fresh and familiar. I find a big stone from behind the hut and place it on top to mark the space. Nearby I burn a candle in the midst of tiny green spring shoots. Suddenly snow falls lightly. It is a peaceful moment. I will leave when the candle burns out.

> *I embrace this earth*
> *all creatures*
> *who live upon it.*

I go to the river and release the braid into the rushing water.

> *I am grateful*
> *for life*
> *ever moving*
> *ever changing*
> *Life.*

April 7, 1985
The River House

Recovering from this most difficult and most dangerous round of visions is demanding great time and patience. Sleeping, eating, moving at all is a great challenge. I am unable to be alone, especially at night. I fear that the energy will dip in and pull me away, killing me while I sleep. So many people are helping me. I do not know what I would do without them. Today I experience, for the first time, safety in my sleeping, outside, under a tree by the river.

I make applesauce. I wash the apples, quarter them, core, peel, and slice them. And I stir. I stir and stir. Mostly I walk. I walk every time I feel pulled away. Slowly I witness the increments of my realignment. I walk and walk and begin to be hungry. I am safe if I can keep my eyes open, stay present. I feel most safe and free alone, yet I need others to help me. Sometimes I walk two to three hours a day. I still cannot read, really. I take no baths and never light candles.

My last effort has been to let go of even hoping that this experience might have value or meaning in my life or in the lives of others. Yesterday I surrendered to that too, surrendering to absolute nothingness. Since then, I am better. There is no past, no future, no hope. Infinity is now. The simplest activities are miraculous. There is no reality other than the present, and the present is whole. I know it directly.

EPILOGUE

()

Re-entry into the world was awkward and extremely demanding. My
fragility required strict adherence to my tremendous need for protection
from most foods and most people, from traffic, from noise, from
information about ways in which to rebuild my life. Within the austerity
of such carefully measured external stimulation, the internal process of
return evolved.

As an initiate, I had learned through trial and error never to interfere
with the energy on its path, only to develop a respectful relationship to
it. Likewise, in returning, I knew that I must not try to integrate such a
force, knowing in my bones that it would integrate itself. Within my
developing relationship with Theo, my commitments continued to be
mothering David and Zachary, strengthening my body by constant
attention to diet and rest, and clarifying the relationship between
surrender and will regarding my experience of the energy.

Enactment of private ritual, which I learned and developed within the
initiation itself, created a container for the journey back into life. I soon

realized that I could again safely choose to see visions, either in response to the familiar signs of the impending energy or if I felt that it was the correct time. The content of the visions was a weave of some of the original themes and rhythms apparent in the initiation, with new symbols and sensations arising from the continuing and extraordinary changes in my perception of reality.

I received more visions concerning my relationship to the suffering in the world and to the cycles, the infinite cycles, of birth and death moving through me. At the same time recurrent visions of wholeness, in my body and in the universe, brought me great and deep peace. A few years ago the image of my final guide—a specific image of myself— integrated, creating an experience of union. In the process of my return, integration becomes an experience of union with the energy itself. Time passes, years pass, and less and less frequently the energy happens to me. The energy is becoming me, and often the energy is me. Originally the energy brought me into experience of the sacred. Now, as the energy integrates with my being, being is sacred.

Gradually, the passion, the fire, the utter vividness of image and the concomitant impact on my body, faded. I mourned the loss and at the same time felt profound relief as well as wonder in the development of my new life. Vision retreats became less frequent and I engaged in the outer world with more strength and endurance. The sensation of emptiness within my body and my mind became increasingly manifest and I longed for its reflection around me.

There have been some exceptions in these years of increasing emptiness. Occasionally I see visions, visions etched in the brilliant light, visions that feed my soul. And perhaps my intimate relationship with fire will be with me always. When there is an abundance of fire somewhere in the world, I find myself spontaneously withdrawing from the external world and moving into the visionary state. During the 1989 California earthquake and the Persian Gulf War in 1991, I received extremely demanding visions in which I experienced my body as a conduit for souls released during those shifts in human consciousness.

Recently, while preparing this text for publication, the fire has reappeared quite differently. The flame is no longer yellow-orange, no longer white, but now clear, transparent. The energy repeatedly moves in the rhythm of labor, not contracting, but instead moving as a snake moves, undulating through my neck and out the top of my head.

This undulating curve exquisitely becomes the rushing, narrow river, the one into which I was pulled by the silver ring fifteen years ago. The river now runs between the edge of my initiatory journey and the edge of my culture. In a vision, I see that I must cross a delicately formed bridge that reaches over this river. With all of me, every cell concentrating, focusing on specific tasks, I move the energy from my body across the bridge to the collective body. The tasks completed, I become the bridge, arching backward over the ever-changing, dynamic force.

> **[()]** *Now I see*
> *the silver ring*
> *closer to the front*
> *of my mouth*
> *radiating light*
> *glowing.*
> *Transparent forms*
> *roll*
> *out through the top*
> *of the ring.*
> *My voice?*

Discovering my new voice, contained by the silver ring, invites consciousness concerning an ancient fear, enabling me to better understand my original need to publish this text under a pseudonym. Fear of the power of another voice lives within me, within the history of my woman's body, within the history of my Western psyche. Men and women have struggled with that voice, feared, obeyed, and disobeyed it, for as long as they have struggled with the dark side of the matriarchy.

◖◗ Sand is the ground.
Out of the sand
emerging up and
toward me
I see three
great fossils, men
clearly the patriarchy
of the synagogue
of the church
of the ashram.

These men look
exactly alike, crumbling
full of holes
fragile, indeed
fossils. Bearded
and with thin voices
they speak to me
but I cannot understand
their words. I see them
reaching slowly
a hand toward
my mouth.

They intend to silence
my voice. My words
my embodied experience
challenge, interrupt
confuse the order
of ancestral
theological structures.

Seeing these men and thus embodying them reduces their power
instantly. It no longer matters what name I use. I am free.

Now comes the dusk. I have been waiting all day. Feeling gratitude for the hot water, for the light shifting, for the gift of my journey, I step in. As I sit down, I am my clear self, no longer separate from my personality.

[(] *I write*
my given name
slowly, carefully

I bend my arms, holding my hands up, open. I hear so clearly the sounds of the universe—all creatures, all beings, one sound, strong and delicate. I notice now my elbows are banging the sides of the tub, sounding like big bells, ringing in celebration. I lie back down into the water.

[(] *I see* Arching Backward
floating along
the narrow river
rushing
toward the left.
The silver ring
loops
through the pages
of the book
from top to bottom
protecting
washing down a page

out and then back
down and through
a simple
a clear way of knowing.

I get out of the tub, looking through the glass doors into the night.

[0] *I see an arc*
the bottom third
of a shallow bowl.
Not reaching very high
on either side
it lies open
wide, almost flat
on the bottom.

This arc glows
warm, a hope
a new vessel
to receive others
who take their turn
after me
seeing
hearing and knowing
becoming
bringing full-bodied
themselves
because of the fire
into the vast body
of the collective.

May this arc, this vessel, welcome—hold—correctly receive initiates
returning.

Now I see my body
not male
not female, curled
arching forward
becoming the soft
stone of alabaster
lying down
so small
in the very center
of the arc
the wide embrace.

My journey
complete, I lay
down this burden.
I lay down
this gift.